VOICES IN LITERATURE

Mary Lou McCloskey • Lydia Stack

Heinle & Heinle Publishers • An International Thomson Publishing Company • Boston, Massachusetts 02116 U.S.A.

I(T)P

The publication of *Voices in Literature Gold* was directed by the members of the Heinle & Heinle Secondary ESL Publishing Team:

Editorial Director: Roseanne Mendoza
Senior Production Services Coordinator: Lisa McLaughlin
Market Development Director: Ingrid Greenberg

Also participating in the publication of this program were:

Vice President and Publisher: Stanley J. Galek
Director of Production: Elizabeth Holthaus
Senior Assistant Editor: Sally Conover
Manufacturing Coordinator: Mary Beth Hennebury
Project Management/Composition/Design: Hispanex, Inc.

Cover art: Rufino Tamayo, "Man and Woman" (Hombre y Mujer), 1981

ISBN: 0-8384-7035-1
Manufactured in the United States of America.

Heinle & Heinle
An International Thomson Publishing Company
Boston, Massachusetts 02116 U.S.A.

13   14   04   03   02   01

Dedicated to the memory of Beverly A. Benson
—consummate professional, valued colleague,
and treasured friend.

The authors and publishers would like to acknowledge the contributions of the following individuals who reviewed and field-tested *Voices in Literature Gold* at various stages of development and who offered many helpful insights and suggestions.

Reviewers

Linda Sasser
Alhambra School District (CA)

Miriam Whitney
Littleton High School (CO)

Mercedes Cohen
El Monte High School (CA)

Molly Anderson
Port Charlotte Middle School (FL)

Joni Beebe
Independence High School, San Jose (CA)

Elaine M. Caret
Burlingame High School (CA)

Charles Glassman
International High School at
La Guardia Community College
Long Island City (NY)

Jim Burke
Burlingame High School (CA)

Celeste De Coudres
Los Angeles Unified School District

Cynthia Cosgrave
Portland Public Schools (OR)

Field–testers

Chris Pehl
Balboa High School, San Francisco (CA)

Sharolyn Hutton
Newcomer School at Chaffey Unified
    School District, Ontario (CA)

Yvette St. John
Jefferson High School, Portland (OR)

Elizabeth Hartung-Cole
Long Beach Unified School District (CA)

Arlene Rotter
Newton County Schools, Covington (GA)

Acknowledgments

The authors would like to thank our husbands, Joel Reed and Jim Stack, for their all-around support as treasure hunters, listeners, readers, advice-givers, chefs, and bottle washers. We are also grateful to our children, Erin, Deirdre, Sean, Kevin, and Tom for their interest, patience, and understanding during our sometimes lengthy coast-to-coast trips and conversations.

We thank all our reviewers, piloters, and their students for their enthusiastic responses to the literature and activities in this book and for their constructive suggestions for improvement.

Jodi Cressman, Sherrie Tindle, and Michael Boomershine provided invaluable help in creating the manuscript; we are most appreciative of them all.

Finally, we gratefully acknowledge Heinle & Heinle Publishers for listening to ESOL teachers and responding with the beautiful, accessible, and challenging series that our students need and deserve.

(continued on p. 254)

Welcome to *Voices in Literature Gold.* This book was written so that you, students from many cultures and language backgrounds, could learn English, talk about literature, and explore themes that are found in many cultures. We have tried to find selections that will help you understand North American culture, selections about moving from one culture to another, and selections that reflect the many cultures that make up North America. We hope that some of the selections will remind you of experiences and stories of your families and friends.

Many of the activities in the book are meant to be done in pairs or small groups. You will work with other students to solve problems and design projects that reflect not only your own thinking, but also new ideas you and your classmates will discover by working in groups. In most cases, there is no one right answer or one way to do an activity. You will have choices to make, and the products will reflect your own creativity and hard work.

You will need to expand the English you use so that you can talk about the literature, find out what it means to you, and make others understand your point of view. You will learn new language from the authors, your teachers, and your fellow students.

In the first unit, *Style,* you will address the discovery and development of self through choices made about style. The second unit, *Suspense,* examines scary stories from all over the world. Unit Three is about the universal human experience of *Love.* Unit Four, *Advice,* contains selections that help you explore issues of what is important and honest in life.

We hope you enjoy *Voices in Literature Gold.* We would love to hear your ideas and opinions about it.

Mary Lou McCloskey
Lydia Stack

Voices in Literature Gold provides teachers and students of English for speakers of other languages (ESOL) an anthology of high-quality literature. The selections and the activities for using those selections will help students interact with literature to benefit their language learning, to foster literary discussion, and to introduce to students the language and concepts of literature. A variety of ways for teachers and students to approach the literature selections, to interact with the actual texts, and to respond to the selections have been included.

Some of your students may have used the companion to this book, *Voices in Literature Silver.* Others may have had less exposure to literature and literary discussion. We have therefore chosen selections and created activities to suit the range of backgrounds of your multi-level class.

Why use literature?

Literature is an appropriate, valuable, and valid medium to assist ESOL students in accomplishing important goals. Literature provides students with motivation to learn and models of high-quality language while it enhances students' imagination, interaction, and collaboration.

Motivation. Literature motivates students by touching on themes they care about, such as love, fear, changes, and hopes for the future. Good literature is about the human experience; it is meaningful to students from different linguistic and cultural backgrounds.

Models. Carefully chosen literature provides models of high-quality language with sophistication and complexity appropriate to students' age levels. Literature offers new vocabulary in context and serves as a source for learning about the mechanics of language in authentic contexts, as they are used by masters of that language.

Imagination. Imagination is one of the abilities that makes us fully human. Literature can give students the means to imagine and think creatively. Literature demands that the reader step into the author's world; good literature demands thought from the reader. Students who are learning a new language need and deserve the challenges to their imaginations that appropriate literature provides.

Interaction and collaboration. Language is learned best in a setting in which it is put to use. Literature provides a common text from which students can negotiate meaning. Well-selected literature addresses issues that are vital to young readers and that stimulate lively discussion among students. Using literature in combination with collaborative activities helps students to better understand the literature, to relate it to their own ideas and experiences, and to go beyond the literature to produce their own literature-related creations.

What kinds of literature should be used?

In selecting texts for *Voices in Literature Gold* we have used a broad definition of literature and have included fiction, nonfiction, poetry, drama, and folktales. We sought authentic and rich texts that provide high-quality language models. We feel that there is no need to "water down" the literature we use with ESOL students; we just need to choose it carefully. In making selections, we were also guided by the following concerns:

Student interest. Literature should be age-appropriate and should address themes of interest to the learners.

Linguistic accessibility. The language of the literature should be clear and simple enough for students to understand, yet it must be expressive, figurative, and evocative to match the maturity and intellectual sophistication of the students. We have included, for example, many poetry selections. Poetry is simple—often using rhyme, rhythm, and repetition to enhance comprehensibility—yet also complex, evoking deep emotion and thought in the reader.

Cultural relevance. Literature selected for ESOL students should reflect many cultures, address concerns of individuals who are experiencing cultural change, and teach about the new, English-speaking culture.

How can literature be used effectively in the ESOL classroom?

We have used a variety of strategies and structures to support students as they learn language through literature and study literature through language. Thematic organization offers students the opportunity to relate concepts and works of literature to one another. The revisitation of themes, ideas, and terms provides enhanced context and thus improves comprehensibility. The supportive format we offer follows an "into-through-beyond" model that includes activities for use before, during, and after reading the literature.

Before you read. We use activities and discussion that connect students' own experience to the literary selection they will read, and we provide background information about the literature to guide them "into" the work.

The selection. We provide a variety of ways to guide students "through" the work, including activities such as reading aloud to students, shared reading, supportive questions during reading, dividing the reading into manageable "chunks," and cooperative learning activities.

After you read. Finally, we use thought-provoking discussion questions, cooperative learning activities, experiences to expand comprehension of literary concepts and terms, writing activities, project ideas, and suggested further readings to take students "beyond" the work into their own high-level thinking and original creations. Many activities employ graphic organizers and learning strategies that can be adapted for use in many other learning situations. At the end of each unit, we include activities to help students relate the works to one another around the unit themes.

Appendices. At the end of the book there are three Appendices that will be useful to you and your students.

Appendix A is a literary appendix that includes the remaining stanzas of *The Raven,* and *Act II, Scene 2 of Romeo and Juliet.* Excerpts from these selections appear in the text of the book. You and your students may decide whether you prefer to read the entire selection or the portion in the unit.

Appendix B is a *Guide to Literary Terms and Techniques* that are discussed in the *Learning About Literature* sections from *Voices in Literature Gold.*

Appendix C is an alphabetic glossary of the vocabulary annotated in the text.

We hope that you and your students enjoy using the selections and activities in *Voices in Literature Gold,* and that they enrich your classroom learning community. We would love to hear from you and your students about your experiences with *Voices.*

Table of Contents

Unit 1: Style

Unit 2: Suspense

Unit 4: Advice

Walk on the Bridge by August Macke, 1912

U N I T

1

Style

What we wear can reveal a
lot about us. We can also
learn about ourselves by
examining how we think and
feel about clothing. The
literature selections in this
first unit are related by their
concern with style. In a deeper
sense, they address the
discovery and development of
self through choices made
about style.

➤ *Exploring Your Own Experience*

Ask-Draw-Pair-Share

What clothing did your parents, grandparents, and great-grandparents wear when they were young? Where did they live? How did they make a living? In what way was their lifestyle different from yours?

1. At home, ask older family members the questions above.
2. Draw pictures, bring photographs, or write short descriptions of how your family members answer your questions.
3. At school, share your pictures and answers with a classmate.
4. You and your partner can join another pair of classmates, and each person can tell his or her partner's story.
5. Some students may wish to share their pictures and descriptions with the whole class.

➤ *Background*

The author of this poem is a Canadian Chippewa Indian. The Chippewa, also called the Anishinabe or Ojibwa, once lived in the forest country around the shores of Lake Superior and were skilled at fishing, hunting, and gathering wild plants. Today, many Chippewa live on reservations in the north-central United States and south-central Canada. Most, however, live outside reservations. Modern Chippewa have a wide range of professions—in the arts, law, teaching, medicine, hunting, trapping, and agriculture.

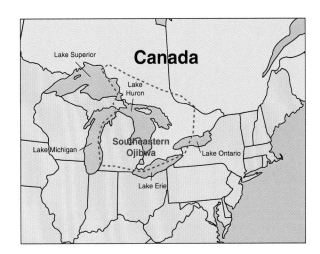

My moccasins have not walked

by
Duke Redbird

My moccasins have not walked
Among the giant forest trees

My leggings have not brushed
Against the fern and berry bush

My medicine pouch has not been filled
with roots and herbs and sweetgrass

My hands have not fondled the spotted fawn

---

fern   a non-flowering plant with feather-shaped leaves
pouch   small bag for carrying things
herbs   plants from which leaves and stems are used as
medicines or seasonings
fondled   stroked, petted

Portrait of an Indian Man by Jack Hokeah

My eyes have not beheld
The golden rainbow of the north

My hair has not been adorned
With the eagle feather

Yet
My dreams are dreams of these
My heart is one with them
The scent of them caresses my soul

....

adorned decorated, made pretty
caresses touches lovingly

ABOUT THE AUTHOR

Duke Redbird, a Canadian Chippewa poet, has served as an independent T. V. producer, actor, writer, carnival side–show performer, wilderness guide, politician, and advocate for Canadian Native People.

➤ **Duke Redbird (born 1939)** ◄

➤ *What Do You Think?*

Think about the poem and discuss your ideas with your classmates and your teacher. Below are some ideas and questions to talk about. Whenever you can, refer back to the text of the poem to check your ideas and answers.

1. Try to retell this poem in your own words. Your teacher may ask you to work with a partner or a small group to retell one line or a group of lines from the poem.

2. The poet talks about the things he did not wear and did not do. Who do you think wore and did these things? Support your ideas using lines from the poem.

3. Many times, poets write about one thing to describe another. In this poem, the poet mentions only particular things, such as moccasins, leggings, medicine pouch, and eagle feather. Do you think the poet could be talking about something bigger? What could that be?

➤ *Try This* AM

Summarizing Information on a Chart

Summarize the information from the activity you did before reading this poem. Make a three-column chart comparing yourself, your parents, and your grandparents. Use key words, not sentences. Try to include many specific words and details.

Styles of Generations

	What clothing did they wear?	*Where did they live?*	*How did they make a living?*
My family			
My parents' families when they were young			
My grandparents' families when they were young			

➤ Learning About Literature

Repetition (AM)

One way poets make sure that their words stay in the reader's memory is by using *repetition*. For example, the poet begins four of the stanzas with "My _____ have/has not _____." Are other words, phrases, patterns, or parts of speech (nouns, pronouns, prepositions, and so on) repeated in the poem? If so, find and list them.

➤ Writing

Try to write a poem about your own ancestors using the pattern of this poem, shown below. If you prefer, make up your own pattern to follow.

"My _____ have/has not _____

_____"

To help you get ideas and words for your writing, use information from your drawings, from the stories you shared in pairs, and from your "Styles of Generations" chart.

➤ Exploring Your Own Experience

Do a Quickwrite

A *quickwrite* is an activity to help you experience the fun and pleasure of writing while you begin to organize your thoughts about a topic. To do this, write your thoughts as they come to you. Try writing about an embarrassing moment. Follow these steps:

1. Think about a time when you were embarrassed. What happened? How did you feel?
2. For five to ten minutes, write everything that comes into your head about this embarrassing experience. Write down as many ideas as you can, without worrying about writing correctly. You can correct your grammar, spelling, and punctuation later.

➤ Background

The following selection reads very much like a *memoir*, a recollection of an earlier life experience. As you read, try to decide when the author is writing in her "younger" voice and when she is writing in an "older" voice, looking back with the wisdom of experience.

Eleven

**From *Woman Hollering Creek*
by Sandra Cisneros**

What they don't understand about birthdays and what they never tell you is that when you're eleven, you're also ten, and nine, and eight, and seven, and six, and five, and four, and three, and two, and one. And when you wake up on your eleventh birthday you expect to feel eleven, but you don't. You open your eyes and everything's just like yesterday, only it's today. And you don't feel eleven at all. You feel like you're still ten. And you are—underneath the year that makes you eleven.

Like some days you might say something stupid, and that's the part of you that's still ten. Or maybe some days you might need to sit on your mama's lap because you're scared, and that's the part of you that's five. And maybe one day when you're all grown up maybe you will need to cry like if you're three,

and that's okay. That's what I tell Mama when she's sad and needs to cry. Maybe she's feeling three.

Because the way you grow old is kind of like an onion or like the rings inside a tree trunk or like my little wooden dolls that fit one inside the other, each year inside the next one. That's how being eleven years old is.

You don't feel eleven. Not right away. It takes a few days, weeks even, sometimes even months before you say Eleven when they ask you. And you don't feel smart eleven, not until you're almost twelve. That's the way it is.

Only today I wish I didn't have only eleven years rattling inside me like pennies in a tin Band-Aid box. Today I wish I was one hundred and two instead of eleven because if I was one hundred and two I'd have known what to say when Mrs. Price put the red sweater on

The Reader by Henri Matisse, 1906

my desk. I would've known how to tell her it wasn't mine instead of just sitting there with that look on my face and nothing coming out of my mouth.

"Whose is this?" Mrs. Price says, and she holds the red sweater up in the air for all the class to see. "Whose? It's been sitting in the coatroom for a month."

"Not mine," says everybody. "Not me."

"It has to belong to somebody," Mrs. Price keeps saying, but nobody can remember. It's an ugly sweater with red plastic buttons and a collar and sleeves all stretched out like you could use it for a jump rope. It's maybe a thousand years old and even if it belonged to me I wouldn't say so.

Maybe because I'm skinny, maybe because she doesn't like me, that stupid Sylvia Saldívar says, "I think it belongs to Rachel." An ugly sweater like that, all raggedy and old, but Mrs. Price believes her. Mrs. Price takes the sweater and puts it right on my desk, but when I open my mouth nothing comes out.

"That's not, I don't, you're not… Not mine," I finally say in a little voice that was maybe me when I was four.

"Of course it's yours," Mrs. Price says. "I remember you wearing it once." Because she's older and the teacher, she's right and I'm not.

Not mine, not mine, not mine, but Mrs. Price is already turning to page thirty-two, and math problem number four. I don't know why but all of a sudden I'm feeling sick inside, like the part of me that's three wants to come out of my eyes, only I squeeze them shut tight and bite down on my teeth real hard and try to remember today I am eleven, eleven. Mama is making a cake for me for tonight, and when Papa comes home everybody will sing Happy birthday, happy birthday to you.

But when the sick feeling goes away and I open my eyes, the red sweater's still sitting there like a big red mountain. I move the red sweater to the corner of my desk with my ruler. I move my pencil and books and eraser as far from it as possible. I even move my chair a little to the right. Not mine, not mine, not mine.

In my head I'm thinking how long till lunchtime, how long till I can take the red sweater and throw it over the schoolyard fence, or leave it hanging on a parking meter, or bunch it up into a little ball and toss it in the alley. Except when math period ends Mrs. Price says loud and in front of everybody, "Now,

Rachel, that's enough," because she sees I've shoved the red sweater to the tippytip corner of my desk and it's hanging all over the edge like a waterfall, but I don't care.

"Rachel," Mrs. Price says. She says it like she's getting mad. "You put that sweater on right now and no more nonsense."

"But it's not—"

"Now!" Mrs. Price says.

This is when I wish I wasn't eleven, because all the years inside of me—ten, nine, eight, seven, six, five, four, three, two, and one—are pushing at the back of my eyes when I put one arm through one sleeve of the sweater that smells like cottage cheese, and then the other arm through the other and stand there with my arms apart like if the sweater hurts me and it does, all itchy and full of germs that aren't even mine.

That's when everything I've been holding in since this morning, since when Mrs. Price put the sweater on my desk, finally lets go, and all of a sudden I'm crying in front of everybody. I wish I was invisible but I'm not. I'm eleven and it's my birthday today and I'm crying like I'm three in front of everybody. I put my head down on the desk and bury my face in my stupid clown-sweater arms. My face all hot and spit coming out of my mouth because I can't stop the little animal noises from coming out of me, until there aren't any more tears left in my eyes, and it's just my body shaking like when you have the hiccups, and my whole head hurts like when you drink milk too fast.

But the worst part is right before the bell rings for lunch. That stupid Phyllis Lopez, who is even dumber than Sylvia Saldívar, says she remembers the red sweater is hers! I take it off right away and give it to her, only Mrs. Price pretends like everything's okay.

Today I'm eleven. There's a cake Mama's making for tonight, and when Papa comes home from work we'll eat it. There'll be candles and presents and everybody will sing Happy birthday, happy birthday to you, Rachel, only it's too late.

I'm eleven today. I'm eleven, ten, nine, eight, seven, six, five, four, three, two, and one, but I wish I was one hundred and two. I wish I was anything but eleven, because I want today to be far away already, far away like a runaway balloon, like a tiny o in the sky, so tiny-tiny you have to close your eyes to see it.

Sandra Cisneros, the daughter of a Mexican father and a Mexican-American mother, grew up in two worlds—traveling between the United States and Mexico, and between Spanish  and English. She writes about conflicts related to growing up between those two worlds—divided loyalties, feelings of not belonging, and the experience of poverty.

> **Sandra Cisneros (born 1954)** ◄

AFTER YOU READ

➤ *What Do You Think?*

Think about the story and discuss your ideas with your classmates and your teacher. Below are some other ideas and questions to talk about. Whenever you can, refer back to the text of the selection to check your ideas and answers.

1. Retell the story in your own words. What do you think Rachel is feeling?
2. How does Rachel act many ages at once?
3. Does it sound to you as if an eleven-year-old is speaking in this selection? What details make you think so?
4. How does the fact that it is Rachel's birthday affect the story?
5. Have you ever experienced a situation like Rachel's in which you were the victim of an injustice but were powerless to speak out against it? How does your story compare to Rachel's?

6. With a partner, try to come up with a one-sentence statement of what you think is the *theme,* or main idea, of this selection.

➤ *Try This*

Description by Comparison AM

A *simile* is a comparison in which two things are compared using *like* or *as*. For example, Cisneros writes that "the way you grow old is kind of like an onion." In fact, Cisneros uses the word *like* more than twenty times in this selection. Although she uses the word in other ways too, in many instances the word *like* signals a simile.

Practice making up similes. Look at the pictures below and see if you can imagine something they remind you of. For example, broccoli stalks might remind you of trees; potatoes might remind you of people watching TV.

Food:	Broccoli	Potatoes	Parsley	Mushrooms	Grapes
Reminds me of:	Fallen trees	People watching T.V.			

1. Find every example in which the author uses *like*. You may wish to mark them with bookmarks or self-stick note paper.
2. List all the similes you find in this selection.
3. Do you think the similes in this selection were written by an eleven-year-old narrator? Look over your list to decide.

➤ *Learning About Literature*

Irony

In literature, we use the term *irony* to describe a contrast or a lack of "fit" between what is stated and what the author meant. The contrast could also be between what is expected to happen and what actually happens. Three kinds of irony are *verbal irony, dramatic irony,* and *situational irony.*

- *Verbal irony*—A writer or speaker says one thing and means another. For example, when something bad happens, someone says, "Oh, that's great."
- *Dramatic irony*—The reader or the audience knows something that a character does not know. An example of dramatic irony in the play *Romeo and Juliet* is the moment when Romeo thinks Juliet is dead and kills himself. However, the audience knows that Juliet is still alive.
- *Situational irony*—An event that happens contrasts with what the characters, the readers, or the audience expect. An example of situational irony is a firehouse that was burned down or a police station that was robbed.

1. Which types of irony do you think Cisneros uses in this selection?
2. Find the passages that show her use of irony.

➤ *Writing*

A Childhood Memoir **AM**

Use Sandra Cisneros' selection as a model for writing about an event in your past. The following suggestions may help you.

1. Draw a picture to represent a person with all the different ages inside him or her, as is suggested by Cisneros. A tree trunk or an onion with rings are examples.
2. Label each ring with an age—for example, 3, 6, 9, 12, and 15.
3. For each age, write a few phrases that describe what you might have thought about or acted like at that age.
4. Choose one of the ages. Try to write about an event in your own past from your point of view at that age.

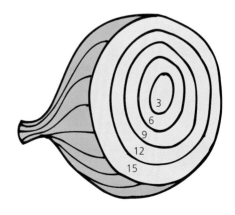

➤ *Exploring Your Own Experience*

Masks **AM**

For many different reasons, people sometimes choose to hide their real feelings. In "Eleven," Rachel was upset because she couldn't hide her feelings and cried in front of the class. Have you ever been in a situation in which you felt like crying, but smiled instead? Have you been in a situation in which you felt angry, but put on a calm face instead?

1. Think about the situation.
2. Discuss your experience with a small group of classmates.
3. Draw two masks to show the way you felt and the face you showed.
4. You may choose to share your masks with the class and put them in a class display.
5. Discuss the different reasons people choose to wear masks. Is it helpful or harmful to wear masks?

➤ *Background*

As you read the following poem, think about how and why people choose to hide their feelings.

We Wear the Mask

by
Paul Laurence Dunbar

We wear the mask that grins and lies,
It hides our cheeks and shades our eyes—
This debt we pay to human guile;
With torn and bleeding hearts we smile,
And mouth with myriad subtleties.

Why should the world be overwise,
In counting all our tears and sighs?
Nay, let them only see us, while
      We wear the mask.

---

grins   smiles widely
guile   trickery
myriad   countless, many
subtleties   ways that are indirect, not open or easily
detected

Les Fetiches by Lois Maitou Jones, 1938

We smile, but, O great Christ, our cries
To thee from tortured souls arise.
We sing, but oh the clay is vile
Beneath our feet, and long the mile;
But let the world dream otherwise,
      We wear the mask!

....

tortured   hurt, tormented
vile   hateful

➤ *What Do You Think?*

Think about the poem and discuss your ideas with your classmates and your teacher. Below are some other ideas and questions to talk about. Whenever you can, refer to the text of the poem to check your ideas and answers.

1. What does the mask of the poem look like?
2. What does this mask hide? From whom does the mask hide the wearer?
3. Why do you think "we" wear the mask?
4. Who do you think are the "we" of the poem?
5. Does it help or hurt to wear the mask? Support your answer with lines or ideas from the poem.
6. Did reading about Paul Laurence Dunbar change your ideas about the poem? If so, in what way?

➤ *Learning About Literature*

Meter

Meter is a pattern of rhythm that repeats itself over and over in a line of writing. When an author uses a line of words that have a regular rhythm, the author is using meter. An example of the use of meter from Dunbar's poem is, "We wear the mask that grins and lies/ It hides our cheeks and shades our eyes." Can you find two other clear examples of the use of meter in "We Wear the Mask?"

Rhyming Couplets

Rhyme is the use of similar sounds in words or phrases that appear close to one another in a poem. Most rhymes occur on the final syllable of the last word on a line.

A *rhyming couplet* is two lines of a poem that rhyme at the end of each line:

> *Twinkle, twinkle little star*
> *How I wonder what you are.*

Rhyme can be a way to enhance how a poem sounds, as it does in "We Wear the Mask."

➤ Try This

Finding the Rhyme AM

Try these activities and discussion questions to begin to increase your understanding of rhyme. Later in the book, you will learn more about rhyme.

1. Find every pair and group of rhyming words in "We Wear the Mask."
2. Where do these words appear? What is their pattern?
3. Label each rhyme with a letter, starting with *a*, then *b*, then *c*, and so on (see example below).
4. List the letter of the rhyme of each line. This is the *rhyme scheme,* or pattern of the poem. Did you notice the pattern before doing this exercise?
5. Discuss what effect these rhyming words have. Do they make the poem easier to remember? Do they mark sections of the poem to give it a clearer structure?

Rhyme Scheme for First Stanza of
"We Wear the Mask"

lies	*a*
eyes	*a*
guile	*b*
smile	*b*
subtleties	*c*

➤ Writing

Rhyming Couplets AM

Write a rhyming couplet about a time you "wore a mask" or about another topic you choose.

1. Review what you wrote or drew about masks before you read the poem. Then reread the poem. Close your eyes and search for an image or a picture in your mind that you would like to write about.
2. Share your ideas with a small group of classmates. Have the group help you think of as many rhyming words related to your topic as they can.
3. Draft your rhyming couplet.
4. Share your couplets with your group and give one another feedback. Try one of the following strategies:
   a. *Encouragement.* Show interest. Tell the poets what you like about the couplets.
   b. *Questions.* Ask questions to help you to get more information or to help you understand better.
   c. *Suggestions.* Suggest ideas but make it clear that the poets may take or leave any suggestions they wish.
5. Revise your couplet.
6. Volunteers may wish to read their revised couplets to the class.

➤ *Exploring Your Own Experience*

Favorite Clothes Interview and Tally AM

1. Interview a partner about his or her favorite article of clothing. Ask your partner questions like these:

   • What is your favorite article of clothing?
   • Can you please describe it?
   • How did you get it?
   • When do you wear it?
   • Why do you like it so much?

2. Share what your partner told you with a small group or with the class.

3. Make a class tally of which articles of clothing most students prefer. Then design a graph like the one below to show the results of the tally.

Favorite Clothes			
Shirt	Pants	Shoes	Hat
II	IIII	̶H̶H̶ I	̶H̶H̶ IIII

➤ *Background*

The following reading is called an *ode,* a special form of poetry that praises someone or something enthusiastically. The ancient Greeks wrote three-part choral odes as parts of plays. They also wrote odes in praise of athletic heroes. Poets throughout history have written odes in praise of famous people, works of art, and nature's power and beauty. The author of this ode comes from Chile in South America.

Chile

Ode to my Socks

by Pablo Neruda
(Translation by Robert Bly)

Maru Mori brought me
a pair
of socks
which she knitted herself
with her sheepherder's hands,
two socks as soft
as rabbits.
I slipped my feet into them
as though into
two cases
knitted
with threads of
twilight
and goatskin.
Violent socks,
my feet were two fish made
of wool,
two long sharks,
sea-blue, shot
through by one golden thread,
two immense blackbirds,

....

immense   very big

Illustration by H. Bonner

two cannons
my feet
were honored
in this way
by these
heavenly
socks.
They were
so handsome
for the first time
my feet seemed to me
unacceptable
like two decrepit
firemen, firemen
unworthy
of that woven
fire,
of those glowing
socks.

Nevertheless
I resisted
the sharp temptation
to save them somewhere
as schoolboys
keep
fireflies,

....

cannons   very large guns that shoot
iron balls
decrepit   old, falling apart
temptation   desire to do something
one shouldn't do

as learned men
collect
sacred texts,
I resisted
the mad impulse
to put them
into a golden
cage and each day give them
birdseed
and pieces of pink melon.
Like explorers
in the jungle who hand
over the very rare
green deer
to the spit
and eat it
with remorse,
I stretched out
my feet
and pulled on the magnificent
socks
and then my shoes.

....

impulse   sudden urge to do something
spit   stick used for cooking meat
over an open fire
remorse   sorrow, regret
magnificent   very grand, impressive

The moral
of my ode is this:
beauty is twice
beauty
and what is good is doubly
good
when it is a matter of two
socks
made of wool
in winter.

....

moral message, meaning

AFTER YOU READ

➤ *What Do You Think?*

Think about the poem and discuss your ideas with your classmates and your teacher. Below are some other ideas and questions to talk about. Whenever you can, refer back to the text of the poem to check your ideas and answers.

1. In this ode, Neruda debates whether or not to wear his new socks. How do you think he feels when he chooses not to wear them?
2. How does he feel when he chooses to put them on?
3. To what does he compare his feet when he wears his socks?
4. Do you think socks are an unusual subject for an ode? If so, what do you think are good subjects for this type of poem?

5. How does this poem make you feel?
6. Now that you have read an ode, how would you define one?
7. Do you usually associate socks with beauty? How does Neruda connect the two?

➤ *Try This*

Cluster Map AM

Bring or wear a favorite article of clothing or a favorite object to school. Look at it very carefully, noting all its details. Think of other things this article reminds you of. Then make a cluster map of words that describe this article. First, write the name of your article or object in the middle of the map. Then, around it, write words that describe it. Connect related words with lines. An example follows.

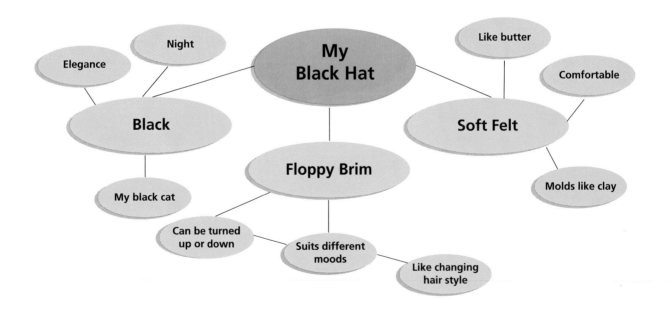

➤ *Learning About Literature*

Rhythm in Poetry

1. Work in small groups.
2. Each group chooses a favorite section of the poem—about five or six lines. Each group member should make a copy of that section.
3. Listen to someone read "Ode to my Socks" or listen to a tape of the poem. Mark with a pencil the stressed and unstressed syllables you hear. Mark *stressed* syllables—ones that sound a little louder and clearer—with " ′ ". Mark *unstressed* syllables—ones that are softer and faster—with " ˘ ".
4. In your group, compare your markings and come to agreement for each line.
5. Read the poem aloud together, accenting the marked syllables.
6. Discuss the patterns you can find in the poem. How can the words or syllables you accent change the meaning of a poem? The first few lines of "Ode to My Socks" might look like this with stress marks:

> Márŭ Mórĭ broúght mĕ
> ă páir
> ŏf sócks
> whĭch shĕ kníttĕd hĕrsélf
> wĭth hĕr shéephĕrdĕr's hánds,
> twó sócks ăš sóft
> ăš rábbĭts.

➤ *Writing* **AM**

Use the words on your cluster map and Neruda's model ode to write your own ode to your favorite article of clothing or object. Read your first draft aloud to your classmates. Revise and edit the ode to create a class book of odes. You might like to illustrate your ode with a drawing, painting, or photograph.

➤ *Exploring Your Own Experience*

Sunshine Outline **AM**

Did you, or someone you know, ever get into trouble by borrowing something? Where were you? Why did you borrow it? Who was with you? What did you borrow? What happened? How did you feel? One way to organize your answers to these questions is with a Sunshine Outline. Follow these three steps:

1. Make an outline like the one below.
2. Write your answers next to the question words in the sun's rays.
3. Discuss your answers with your classmates.

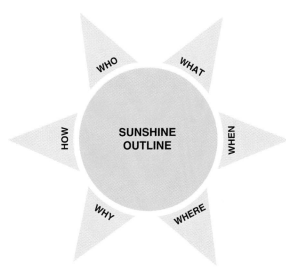

➤ *Background*

Gary Soto writes about the everyday life of young Mexican-Americans in Fresno, California. Soto, like Cisneros, notices details and develops characters to create very engaging, or interesting, stories out of ordinary day-to-day events.

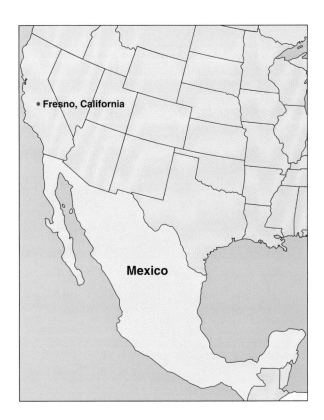

The Raiders Jacket

by
Gary Soto

Lorena Rocha parted the curtain in her living room and looked out onto the wet street. The rain was still coming down but with less wind-blown fury. A shaft of sunlight even appeared, poking through the elm tree at the curb. Lorena smiled and then stopped. The sunlight faltered and disappeared as a cloud once again blocked the sun.

Earlier that Saturday morning it had been coming down, as her father said at breakfast, *como gatos y perros*. If it didn't stop raining soon it would ruin her day. She wanted her mother to drive her to the mall at Fashion Fair, but her mother didn't like to drive in rain—and for a good reason: driving in the rain, she had once gotten into an accident that ripped a mailbox from its cemented bolts.

Lorena and her best friend since first grade, Guadalupe, were desperate to go to the mall. They had to replace a Raiders jacket.

The Wednesday before, Eddie Contreras, the handsomest seventh-grader in their class (if not all of Fresno, California), had given Lorena his jacket to wear.

She has been after Eddie relentlessly since September, and in the second week of October, during lunch, he finally took off his jacket and draped it over Lorena's shoulders. She smiled like a queen. She could feel the warmth

---

faltered   hesitated, stopped for a minute
como gatos y perros   *(Spanish)* like cats and dogs, very hard

relentlessly   without stopping

Photo courtesy of Superstock

of his body in the jacket. Her cheeks blossomed into twin roses of happiness.

"OK, but I want it back tomorrow," he said, walking away with his friend, Frankie Medina, who looked back, winked, and gave Lorena the thumbs-up sign.

"*Qué guapo,*" Guadalupe had said. "I think he likes you."

"Do you think so?" Lorena asked, twirling so that the jacket flared. The sleeves were long and hid her hands. And the collar was as itchy as her father's face at the end of a workday. Still, it was hers for one day. She pushed her hands into the pockets and found a piece of chewing gum, which she tore in half and shared with Guadalupe. It was Juicy Fruit, their favorite.

The two of them were happy and walked around the school yard, parading for all their friends. One girl snapped the gum in her mouth and asked point-blank, "You and Eddie tight?" Lorena didn't answer. Embarrassed, she hid her face behind the sleeves of Eddie's jacket.

When the bell rang Lorena and Guadalupe separated. Lorena went to French class, where she sat warm as a bird in the nest of Eddie's jacket. She went dreamy with deep longing. She kept picturing herself and Eddie running in slow motion down a windswept beach, each of them wearing a Raiders jacket, each of them draped in silver and black. Her smiling face was soft, with a faraway look. When the teacher called on her to conjugate the verb "to swim" in French, Lorena, still lost in her dream, said, "*nado, nadas, nada, nadamos, nadan*"— the Spanish, not the French, conjugation.

During her last class, biology, Lorena overheard a group of whispering girls. One said, "Eddie and Lorena . . . I think they're stuck on each other."

If only it were true, Lorena thought. She hugged herself and felt the warmth of the jacket. For a moment, the beach scene replayed itself in the back of her mind.

The biology teacher made them cut apart dead frogs. He had been telling

---

qué guapo   *(Spanish)* how handsome

conjugate   to list the forms of a verb
nado, nadas, nada, nadamos, nadan *(Spanish)* I swim, you swim *(familiar)*, you swim *(formal)*, or he/she swims, we swim, they swim or you *(all)* swim

them for weeks that they would be dissecting a frog and that they should get used to the idea. He had said that dissecting a frog was no different than cutting apart a barbecued chicken.

"Gross," several of the students said, twisting their faces into ugly knots of disgust.

It *was* gross, Lorena thought. She took the knife in her hand and pierced the skin with a quick jab. She was surprised the frog didn't jump up, open its eyes, look at her, and plead, "Cut it out!"

She removed Eddie's jacket because she didn't want to get blood or gook on it. She folded it and placed it on a chair. Then she returned to dissecting, her face souring when the frog's slit belly opened, revealing a tangle of intestines.

When the bell rang Lorena tossed her half-skinned frog back into a white pan and hurried out of the class. She always had to hurry because the bus she caught for home left promptly ten minutes after school let out. She had to hurry more than usual that day because she had to stop in the office to pick up a release. Her French teacher was taking them to see a movie the next week.

She picked up the form, then raced to board the bus that stood idling in front of the school. The driver was reading a newspaper. His coffee was up on the dash, growing cold.

Lorena waved out the window to Guadalupe, who rode another bus. "I'll call you when I get home," she yelled at her friend, who was pushing a boy who was trying to make her smell his froggy hands.

Lorena found a seat. After a few minutes the driver folded his newspaper, drank his coffee in three gulps, wiped his mouth on his sleeve, and muttered, "Hang on."

The bus lurched and was coughing a black plume of smoke when Lorena looked out the window and saw Eddie and his friend, Frankie, stomping on milk cartons. An explosion of milk burst into the air, scaring two girls who were standing nearby.

Lorena's hands went straight to her shoulders. "The jacket!" she screamed. She shot from her seat and ran up the aisle to the driver.

"You've got to stop! I forgot Eddie's jacket!"

"Who's Eddie? I don't know no Eddie," the driver said, shifting into third. "Sit down."

"I lost his jacket!" she screamed, stomping her foot like a little girl.

---

dissecting   cutting apart to study   **plume**   feather

The driver downshifted as he came to a red light. He turned to her, his lined face dark with stubble. He warned her again with a wag of one ink-stained finger, "I said, sit down."

And she did. She returned to her seat and sat clutching her books. "How can I ever tell Eddie?" she whimpered. She closed her eyes and pictured herself telling him. He was standing by his locker, trying to remember his combination. He wore a T-shirt, the braille of goose bumps on his arms. Outside it was raining hard.

That was Wednesday afternoon. Lorena was frantic that evening when she spoke in hushed tones to Guadalupe on the telephone in the hallway at home.

"How could I be such a *mensa?*" she scolded herself as she sat cross-legged, the telephone cradled in one hand and a cookie in the other. She blamed her biology teacher for her problem. If he hadn't made them dissect frogs, she wouldn't have been so absentminded.

The next day Lorena rushed from the bus to the biology room. The jacket was not there.

"Darn it," she snarled, pounding her fist on a table. She turned angrily and shot a fiery glance at the frogs that had been tossed into the white pan to await first period.

She decided to keep her distance from Eddie by sneaking down the hallways pretending to be reading a book. She spent most of her break and lunch period in the rest room, brushing her hair and worrying. Now and then Guadalupe would come into the rest room to tell her where Eddie was and what he was doing. He had been slap-boxing with Frankie.

Lorena and Guadalupe decided to stay home Friday so that Lorena could

---

stubble   short growth of beard

wag   wave

clutching   holding tightly

whimpered   cried softly

braille   method of writing for the blind that uses raised dots

frantic   very upset, excited

mensa   *(Spanish)* fool

avoid Eddie. She spent the day reading *Seventeen* and eating bowls of saltless popcorn.

The girls decided that they would pool their money and go shopping on Saturday to replace the jacket. Lorena figured she had about eighty dollars, and with Guadalupe's thirty-four dollars, her life savings, they would have enough to buy a new Raiders jacket.

It had been rainy when Lorena awoke Saturday morning, and Guadalupe was really sick but still willing to go with her to Fashion Fair.

"Mom," Lorena called as she walked into the kitchen. "It's stopped raining."

"Did you clean your room?" her mother asked. She was sitting at the kitchen table cutting coupons from the *Fresno Bee* newspaper.

"Two times. I even cleaned the aquarium."

Her mother sighed as she stood. Peeking out the kitchen window, she saw that the rain had let up. It was still misty, but the skinny plum tree they had planted last winter was no longer wavering in the wind. Her mother said, "OK, but you don't have to get me anything fancy."

Lorena had told her mother she wanted to go shopping so that she could buy her a gift for her birthday, which was the next week.

They drove to pick up Guadalupe, who climbed into the car and immediately sneezed. She had a wad of crumpled Kleenex in her fist.

"*Ay*, I bet you got a cold from going outside with your hair wet," Lorena's mother said, accelerating slowly. She didn't want to chance running into a mailbox again.

"I caught a cold from my stupid brother," Guadalupe said. She turned to Lorena and, leaning into her shoulder, whispered, "I got ten more dollars."

They drove in silence to Fashion Fair.

"I don't want you two to fool around," Lorena's mother warned as she let the girls out. She tried to look serious, but both of them knew that she was a softy.

Lorena promised to behave. Guadalupe sneezed and said, "Thank you, Mrs. Rocha. I'll be sure that Lorena doesn't act up."

Lorena pushed Guadalupe, who laughed and said, "Well, I *am* older."

---

wavering   moving back and forth   **accelerating**   speeding up

"But not wiser, *esa*."

The two girls watched the car pull away with Mrs. Rocha gripping the steering wheel with both hands. Then they walked into the mall and headed toward Macy's, which was at the other end. Guadalupe wanted to stop and buy an Orange Julius drink, but Lorena hissed, "Lupe, we may not have enough money!"

"Yeah, you're right," Guadalupe said, stopping to open her purse. She rifled through it—eyeliner, an old report card, gum, sticky Lifesavers, a scrap of paper with the phone number of a so-so-looking boy from Tulare. Her fingers at last squeezed the envelope that contained forty-four dollars. She looked around before handing the envelope to Lorena. "You can pay me back in a month, right?"

"I think I can," Lorena said, her eyes big with excitement. The envelope weighed a lot, and Lorena slipped it into her coat pocket. "Lupe, you're a real friend."

The girls hurried to Macy's, and Lorena thrust her hand into her pocket every now and then to be sure the envelope was still there. They rode the escalator to the second floor and headed for the men's department, where two salesmen were standing near the cash register. They were bent over with laughter, apparently cracking up from a joke. Except for three other shoppers, the department was empty. It was quiet, too, except for the thump of music from an overhead speaker.

Lorena wanted to go unnoticed. She didn't want the salesmen to help. She and Guadalupe slipped past them without being seen and stopped at a rack of Raiders jackets.

"I don't know what size Eddie wears," Lorena said, placing one hand to her chin as she studied the jackets. She took one from the rack and tried it on. The sleeves came down over her hands. "This looks like the size."

"Are you sure?" Guadalupe asked.

"No," she said after a moment. She slipped out of the jacket and looked at the tag inside—size 36. "Guadalupe, try it on."

"Me?" Guadalupe said, pointing a finger tipped with a polished nail at herself.

Guadalupe was an inch taller and twenty pounds heavier than Lorena, a

---

esa *(Spanish)* pal
rifled dug, searched

Bauhaus Stairway by Oskar Schlemmer, 1932

gordita to a *flaca*. She slipped the jacket on, arms outstretched, and asked, "How does it look?"

Lorena squinted and remarked, "I don't know. But I think it's the same size as Eddie's." She scanned the other jackets on the rack. She had to be sure.

"Why don't you just tell Eddie the truth?" Guadalupe suggested." Then he can get his own jacket."

"I'm gonna look like a fool," Lorena said. "I don't want him to know I lost his jacket." She clicked a fingernail against her front teeth and stared at the rack. She stared some more and then replaced the jacket. "I think it was a size 34."

She walked to the cash register with the size 34 jacket. The salesmen were no longer laughing. One was helping a woman who was complaining about a broken zipper, and the other was punching a number into the telephone. When the second salesman saw Lorena, he hung up and asked, "Will this be all?"

"Yeah," she said, her hands shaking. Lorena brought out the envelope and the money from her own purse.

The salesman smiled and said, "Nice jacket. For your boyfriend?" He wagged his head from side to side and smiled, showing his clean, white teeth.

Lorena paid and took the shopping bag from the salesman. "Let's get outta here," she whispered. The two girls rode the escalator down a level and headed for the perfume department, where they dabbed their wrists with the richness of love and passion.

"My mom would like this," Lorena said of a perfume emblazoned with Liz Taylor's signature. "Too bad I don't have enough money."

Neither of the girls was in a good mood. Neither of them liked spending all their money, especially Lorena. She had been saving her money to buy a moped when she turned sixteen and could get her license. Now that dream—*and* the dream of running in slow motion on the beach with Eddie—was dead.

Lorena and Guadalupe left Macy's and were standing in front of Hickory

---

gordita   *(Spanish)* little, chubby girl.
(Note: in Spanish, this is a complementary and affectionate term)
flaca   *(Spanish)* thin girl

dabbed   patted
emblazoned   decorated, displayed very brightly
moped   a bicycle with a motor

Dutch Cheeses, Bread and Knife, artist and date unknown

Farms inhaling the smells of 63 different cheeses and meats when they heard Eddie's voice. They turned and saw Eddie and his friend Frankie, both of whom were devouring bags of popcorn.

"Hey, Lorena, how come you left my jacket in biology?" Eddie asked coolly after he cleared his throat of popcorn. "I thought you liked me."

Lorena nearly fainted. This wasn't a dream. It was a nightmare—in silver and black. Eddie was wearing his Raiders jacket and a sneer on his face.

"Eddie, your jacket," Lorena blurted. She reached out to touch it, but Eddie pulled away. He took a step back and then said to Frankie, "The janitor found my jacket."

"I can explain," Lorena pleaded. "I didn't want to get any frog on your jacket —" Lorena stopped in midsentence. The story sounded ridiculous.

All the while Guadalupe stood staring at her shoes. She saw that her white laces had turned gray and wet from the rain. Her eyes filled with tears for her friend.

---

inhaling breathing in

"Just leave me alone, *esa,*" Eddie said.

Frankie licked his lips and said, "How could you do this to *mi carnal?* Man, he was treating you nice, *loca.*"

After Eddie and Frankie left, chewing their popcorn casually as camels, Lorena and Guadalupe found a quiet place for a good cry. Lorena's tears fell, as her father would say, *como gatos y perros.*

"Eddie will never like me," she sobbed.

"There are bigger fish," Guadalupe comforted her.

They cried into each other's coats, then wiped their eyes and dabbed the buds of their mouths with lipstick. They returned the jacket and bought Lorena's mother some meats and cheeses, not the romantic perfumes called Passion or Ecstasy that filled their noses when they thought of love.

---

mi carnal   *(Spanish)* my brother
loca   *(Spanish)* crazy girl

➤ *What Do You Think?*

Think about the story and discuss your ideas with your classmates and your teacher. Below are some other ideas and questions to talk about. Whenever you can, refer back to the text of the selection to check your opinions and answers.

1. Why do you think Eddie loaned Lorena the jacket? Why was she so happy to borrow it?
2. How would you describe Lorena, Eddie, and Guadalupe? Find passages from the story to back up your descriptions.
3. What is the *climax* of this story—the point at which the reader feels the greatest tension?
4. How did Eddie treat Lorena? Did the experiences with the jacket help Lorena and Guadalupe learn more about Eddie? Do those experiences tell you, the reader, more about Eddie?
5. Why did Lorena choose the gifts she gave to her mother?
6. What do you think Lorena and Guadalupe learned from their experience?

➤ *Try This*

Cause and Effect

An *event* is something that happens in a story. Most of the story takes place in four days— Wednesday, Thursday, Friday, and Saturday. The story begins by telling about Saturday morning, and then there is a *flashback* to Wednesday. The first event happens on Wednesday when Lorena tries to get Eddie to let her wear his Raiders jacket.

1. Divide into groups. Each group is assigned one day of the story.
2. Write the main events of your group's day on index cards or self-stick notes. Use one card or note for each event.
3. Arrange all the cards in the order that the events happened in the story.
4. Look for events that lead to other events. Draw arrows from the *cause* to the *effect*. Remember that the effect of one event can be the cause of another. The example on the next page will help you to get started.

Day: Wednesday

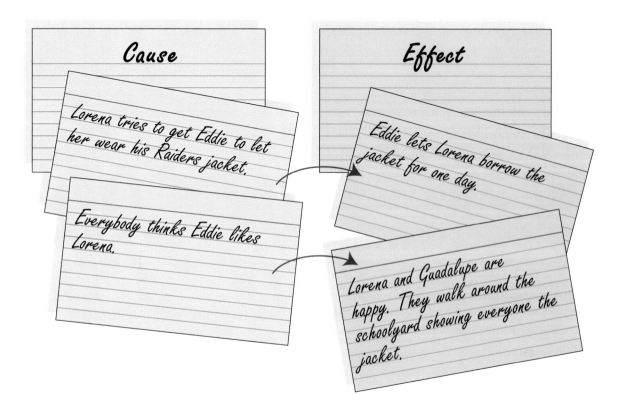

Cause

Lorena tries to get Eddie to let her wear his Raiders jacket.

Everybody thinks Eddie likes Lorena.

Effect

Eddie lets Lorena borrow the jacket for one day.

Lorena and Guadalupe are happy. They walk around the schoolyard showing everyone the jacket.

➤ *Learning About Literature*

Character Development AM

One of the things that makes stories interesting, realistic, and powerful is the way in which the characters change or develop. Use the steps and the model chart on the following page to examine the development of a character in "The Raiders Jacket."

1. Choose a character to analyze or study closely. Choose three qualities of that character to study. Some possible qualities include: kindness, generosity, anger, envy, loyalty, pride, happiness, humility, trust, and hate. Choose a color to represent each quality.

2. Make a chart like the one on the next page. Make a key showing what color represents each quality (see example).

3. Think about what the character you have chosen is like at the beginning of the story. Put the appropriately colored dot above "beginning" for each quality. In the example, the green dot above "beginning," for kindness, is next to "low" because Lorena was less kind at the beginning of the story.

4. Think about what the character is like in the middle of the story and add colored dots above "middle." Do the same above "end" to show the character's qualities at the end of the story.

5. How did the character change or develop? In what ways did the character stay the same? Discuss.

6. Compare your chart with the ones your classmates did for other characters. Decide which characters made important changes and which did not.

➤ *Writing* AM

Choose a character from the story that you think changed in some way during the story. Describe how that character changed and how the events in the *plot,* the main events of the story, contributed to the development of that character. Use quotations from the text to support your ideas.

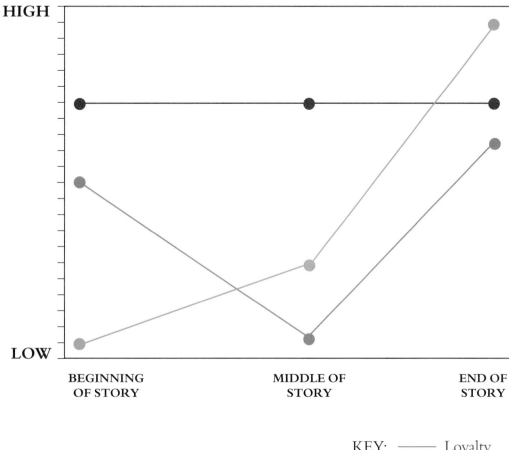

The Development of the Character 'Lorena' in "The Raiders Jacket"

HIGH

LOW

BEGINNING
OF STORY

MIDDLE OF
STORY

END OF
STORY

KEY: —— Loyalty
—— Kindness
—— Pride

➤ Exploring Your Own Experience

Dress Code Interviews `AM`

1. Interview two or three people who have attended more than one school. Ask them about the dress codes of the schools they have attended. Your questions might include the following:

   - What are the names and locations of the schools you have attended?
   - What was the dress code at each school?
   - Were the students required to wear uniforms?
   - What happened if a student didn't follow the dress code?
   - How do you think the dress code affected your behavior and your school work?
   - How did it affect the behavior and school work of other students?

2. Make a class chart to summarize the results of all the interviews. The chart might look like the one below.

3. Summarize the information on your chart. Analyze the information to find answers to questions like these:

   - What percentage of high schools had dress codes?
   - What percentage of students thought wearing uniforms or having dress codes had a good effect on them?
   - What percentage of students thought wearing uniforms or having dress codes had a good effect on other students?

➤ Background

Students at private schools in North America often wear uniforms. Recently, public schools have begun to study the value of school uniforms. The following magazine article examines some of the reasons that schools are choosing uniforms and the success those schools are having in getting students to wear uniforms.

Name and location of school	Uniforms or other dress code?	Consequences of not following code	Effect on student's behavior and school work	Effect on other students' behavior and school work

The Dress Mess

by
Del Stover

School uniforms are finding favor with a small but eager group of educators searching for ways to reduce competition among students enamored of designer jeans, leather jackets, and expensive jewelry. But uniformed students won't be the norm at public schools anytime soon.

Currently, student uniforms are being tried on a voluntary basis in Connecticut, Louisiana, Maryland, New York, and Washington, D.C. In Baltimore, student competition over clothes—plus concern about thieves robbing richly clad students—led that city's school board to require all schools to adopt a voluntary uniform policy.

Most of Baltimore's 118 elementary schools already have students in uniform, says school spokesman Tom Bush: "It's working out fine from the reports we hear. The youngsters seem very proud of the way they look. They seem to come to school prepared for work."

But keeping students in uniform isn't easy. In New Orleans, encouraging use of uniforms has met with mixed success, says Doris Hicks, who

---

competition   one trying to be better than another

enamored of   being very fond of, liking very much

norm   usual way of doing something

currently   at present, now

voluntary   personal choice

clad   dressed

Students at a school near Dar-es Salaam, Tanzania, Africa

chaired the district's uniform study. Although the plan initially met with strong parental support and student compliance, interest has waned, especially among high school students.

Indeed, uniforms often are more successful in the elementary schools, where students are not so intent on their individuality, Hicks says. To date, uniform use varies from 95 percent at

---

initially at first
compliance cooperation, obedience
waned faded, gotten smaller

intent serious about something

Hardin Elementary School, where Hicks is principal, to 50 percent at the high schools.

Most supporters agree a uniform policy won't succeed unless school officials gain the support of a large majority of parents. Nor will success be ensured without vigorous support from the principal. At Hardin, for example, use of uniforms is high largely because Hicks worked closely with parents to design the district-wide policy and then encouraged continued parental support through letters and cheerleading at PTO meetings.

Pushing the economic benefits of school uniforms is a big help in pushing such policies, say supporters. "It started off as a kind of economic necessity," says Baltimore's Bush of the uniform proposal there. "Parents who had a number of children in school found it difficult to dress them, to keep up with the times."

To help cash-strapped parents, the New Orleans Policy allows individual schools to select a basic look for students that is simple in color and style—such as navy blue trousers and skirts, white shirts and blouses, and black shoes—and does not require a specific uniform that would have to be bought from a uniform company. This allows parents to shop for bargains and keeps the promise that school uniforms will be economical, Hicks says.

But what sells principals like Hicks on uniforms is the change in youngsters' attitudes. "I've had fewer difficulties (since the uniforms)," she says. "When the students are in the school yard, they're dressed up, and few kids run around. And we've had fewer discipline problems. I think it's because of the uniforms. They just don't want to get dirty."

---

majority   more than half
vigorous   strong
PTO   Parent-Teacher Organization
economic   financial, money-related
benefits   good results

cash-strapped   with little money
economical   money-saving

AFTER YOU READ

➤ *What Do You Think?*

Think about the article and discuss your ideas with your classmates and your teacher. Below are some other ideas and questions to talk about.

1. Why do you think school leaders and parents see a need for dress codes and uniforms?
2. What benefits do they think dress codes and uniforms bring? Can you think of others?
3. Can you think of any disadvantages of dress codes and uniforms that are not mentioned in the article?
4. Who are the "experts" quoted by the authors? Do you think they are qualified? Who else might the authors have consulted?
5. How do the ideas expressed in this article compare to what you discovered in your interviews and analysis?

➤ *Try This*

Outlining the Article with a Chart **AM**

Outline the article using the following chart. Notice that the author of the article does not draw any conclusions about the dress codes, but only reports on what people think.

1. What is the main idea of this article? (Note: The main idea, or *theme statement*, is not stated in just one sentence, so you will need to use your own words).
2. Make a chart like the one below to find out attitudes about dress codes. Write down the names of four groups of people who have an opinion about the issue, for example, elementary school students, high school students, etc.
3. Complete the chart with details from the article. Find information from the article that shows why each group is in support

Group:	Information in support of wearing uniforms	Information against wearing uniforms
elementary school students		
high school students		
teachers		
parents		

of school uniforms, or why each group is against school uniforms. Write supporting information in the appropriate space. You may not find information for every box.

➤ *Learning About Literature*

News Articles and Essays

The magazine article you just read presents information about dress codes without clearly taking sides. An *essay* usually goes further than a news article. An *essay* is a form of writing in which the writer takes a clear stand on an issue. A *formal essay* is an attempt to inform, teach, or convince the reader. It has a serious tone and presents its arguments logically. An *informal essay* is a lighter piece that usually attempts to entertain the reader and often has a looser structure.

➤ *Writing*

Writing an Essay **AM**

1. Discuss your own ideas about uniforms and dress codes with a small group of classmates. Relate your ideas to the new information that you collected from your interviews and from the article.
2. Use the information from your interviews and your own experiences to outline your own essay on dress codes and uniforms at a particular school.
3. Write a draft of your essay.
4. Share your draft with a small group of classmates.
5. Revise your draft, incorporating ideas from your group discussion.
6. Edit your draft for spelling, usage, punctuation, and so on.
7. Share your writing with others by sending it to an administrator, submitting it to a community or school newspaper or magazine, or sharing it with the whole class.

Unit Follow-Up

➤ *Making Connections*

Unit Project Ideas

Here are some possible unit projects. If you want, think up a project of your own. You can use some of the techniques you learned in this unit to help you plan and complete the project.

1. **Design a Wardrobe.** Using catalogs, select a wardrobe for next season. Draw yourself in some favorite clothes. List the articles you have chosen and their prices and find the total cost. Write about how you will feel in your new wardrobe.

2. **Family Style.** Write about the fashion style of one of your ancestors.

3. **Masks.** Masks are part of the traditions of many cultures. Choose a culture and do research on its masks. Make a mask that shows a traditional style that you studied. Then write an article about masks for your school newspaper or magazine.

4. **School Styles Report.** Use the information you collected on school styles to write a news article about what's "in" and what's "out" this year at your school.

5. **Uniforms Debate.** Hold a class debate on whether or not uniforms would be good for your school. Teams on each side should research their ideas and plan how to best present them.

6. **E-Mail Research.** Use computer message boards to ask for information from other places and cultures about style. Ask correspondents about clothes, music, and language that are in style.

7. **Compare and Contrast Characters.** Study and write about two characters in different selections in this unit—for example, Rachel in "Eleven" and Lorena in "The Raiders Jacket." Compare and contrast these characters. Also compare how the two authors let you find out about their characters.

8. **Favorite Author.** Make a bulletin board about your favorite author from this unit. Read other writings, as well as other biographical information on the author. Tell why this is your favorite author. On your bulletin board, include pictures, quotes, and charts. Also include captions (words or sentences that tell about the pictures, quotes, and charts).

9. Journal. Keep a literary journal of books and selections that you read. For each book or selection, write down the title, author, a short summary, and your response to your readings.

Further Reading

Below are some books related to this unit that you might enjoy.

• *Hear My Voice: A Multicultural Anthology of Literature from the United States,* edited by Laurie King. Addison-Wesley Publishing Co., 1994. This book offers a variety of multicultural writings from around the United States.

• *Local News,* by Gary Soto. Harcourt, Brace, Jovanovich Publishers, 1993. This book of short stories reflects the Mexican-American culture.

• *Neruda and Vallejo: Selected Poems,* edited by Robert Bly. Beacon Press, 1971. All poems in this book are written in both Spanish and English.

• *Red on White: The Biography of Duke Redbird,* by Marty Dunn. Chicago: Follet, 1971. Included in the illustrated story of Duke Redbird's life are many of his poems.

• *The Hundred Dresses,* by Eleanor Estes. Harcourt, Brace, Jovanovich Publishers, 1971. Wanda Petronski wore the same faded-blue dress to school every day. When classmates teased her about her dress, she told them she had "a hundred dresses at home," and it was true.

• *Till All the Stars Have Fallen,* selections by David Booth. Viking Penguin, 1990. David Booth, a professor at the Faculty of Education, University of Toronto, has assembled a charming collection of (mostly) Canadian poetry for young people.

• *Woman Hollering Creek,* by Sandra Cisneros. Random House, Inc., 1991. The author tells short stories about her Mexican-American heritage.

La Bonne Adventure by Rene Magritte, 1954

UNIT

2

Suspense

All over the world, people have told scary stories late in the evening around the fire. These stories have often kept listeners in suspense—sitting "on the edge of their seats," anxiously waiting to find out how the story will end. This unit is full of such stories! So turn down the lights, practice your best ghost-story voices, and prepare to enjoy a unit of suspense!

➤ Exploring Your Own Experience

Wedding and Marriage Customs (AM)

1. Interview your parents or grandparents and ask them to describe some of the traditional wedding customs in their home country.
2. In class, use this information to make a chart of the marriage customs in your country or region. Use the chart below as a guide.
3. Compare your chart with those of other students.

➤ Background

Many Chinese people came to work in California in the early twentieth century. They brought many stories with them, including some about a ghost's bride. As part of a WPA (Works Progress Administration) project in the 1930's, Jon Lee collected and translated tales told in Chinatown in Oakland. Many of these stories originated in the Kwangtung Province of China (now called the Gwangdong Province). Laurence Yep has selected from Jon Lee's stories and retold them in *The Rainbow People*. "The Ghost's Bride" is from this book.

Wedding and Marriage Customs

Who decides who will marry?

What preparations are made for the wedding?

Who pays for what?

What are the wedding ceremonies like?

What kinds of parties are held?

Where do the bride and groom live afterwards?

Typically, how old are the brides and grooms?

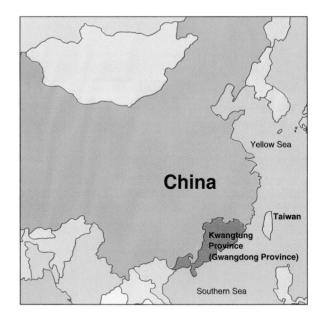

The Ghost's Bride

From *The Rainbow People*
by Laurence Yep

"Come back right away," the mother ordered her daughter. "I will," the girl promised, and she went straight to the next village and did the errand for her mother. But on her way back, the girl began to drag her feet lazily. It was a warm, sunny day, and the girl did not want to go back right away to her chores. So, instead, she sat down on a large, flat stone by a stream and took off her shoes.

At first she splashed her feet happily in the cool water. But then gradually it became harder and harder to wriggle her toes. She thought the water might be too cold so she lifted her feet out to let the sun warm them.

When they still felt stiff, she tried to rub her feet, but she felt nothing. Worse, her ankles and calves were also numb. Worried, she swung her legs from the stone and tried to stand up.

She swayed on her feet, suddenly feeling very tired. She thought about lying down on the stone. It was so pleasant here, and her mean mother worked her too hard. She just needed to rest a moment more.

But in the back of her mind, she felt uneasy. She tried to walk back to her village, but she could barely move her legs. By the time she reached the village gates, her legs were as stiff as sticks.

She collapsed in the dirt, calling for help. The other villagers heard her and

---

errand   short trip for a specific purpose
chores   tasks, jobs around the house
gradually   bit by bit, slowly
wriggle   move back and forth quickly

numb   without feeling
collapsed   fell down

Landscape in the Style of Huang Kung-wang by Wang Yuang chi, 1706

carried her to her house. Her anxious mother put her to bed and did everything she could think of, but the girl's legs became useless. The girl could no longer even walk.

"Did you fall down?" her mother asked.

The girl began to cry. "No."

Puzzled, her mother shook her head. "Something must have happened. You went straight there and back again?"

Through her tears, the girl mumbled, "You'll just scold me."

Her mother stroked her hair just as she had when her daughter was small. "I do scold you. Maybe too much. But that's because I love you."

The girl sniffed. "Well, I did take a little rest."

Her mother kept on stroking her hair. "Where?"

"By the stream near a big flat stone," the girl said.

The worried mother made her daughter comfortable and then retraced her daughter's steps. She even found the stone and the stream. Everything seemed normal.

Completely puzzled now, the mother went to a wise old woman in the next village. The old woman knew how to talk to ghosts.

The wise old woman was laying bundles of herbs out to dry in front of her hut. When the mother told her of their troubles, the wise old woman just shook her head and clicked her tongue. "She sat on the lap of a dead man. Now he wants her for his bride."

"She only sat on a stone," the mother wondered.

"Long ago a farmer died when he was young. A stone marked his grave, but the stone fell over long ago." The old woman went on sadly with her chores. "Beneath the stone lies the man, and beneath the stone that man waits."

But the mother was not about to give up her daughter without a fight. She went back to the stone with bowls of food and a jar of wine for the ghost.

---

anxious worried
retraced went back over

bundles bunches, groups of something tied together
herbs plants from which leaves and stems are used as medicines or seasonings

Night View of Matsuchiyama and the San'ya Canal by Utagawa Hiroshige (1797-1858)

Then she burned special paper money and begged the man to leave her daughter alone.

It was late afternoon by the time she started back for home. Her shadow stretched far behind her like a long, thin puppet. Suddenly she had the feeling that she wasn't alone. When the mother looked behind her, she saw two shadows. The second shadow was that of a man.

"Go away. I don't want a ghost for a son-in-law." She picked up the nearest stone and threw it at the second shadow, and the shadow disappeared.

The mother thought to herself, Maybe I can drive him away from my girl.

So that night the determined mother sat down in a chair and kept watch. In her lap was her big kitchen cleaver. When the shadow appeared on the wall, she waved the cleaver over her head. "I told you to go away."

When the shadow stayed on the wall, the mother struck at the shadow's head and stepped back. To her horror, the head vanished, but the rest of the shadow remained. She struck at the body and the body disappeared. "Go away, go away." Frantically she chopped at the shadow's arms and legs until only the hands and feet were left.

The mother stood panting. Then one hand began to dance like a spider and then the other. The next moment both feet began to leap and hop about. When the head reappeared, the feet began to kick it about like a ball. Finally, the arms, legs, and body appeared. They bounced all about the house.

The mother realized that the ghost was only playing with her. The only damage she had done was to her walls. And in the morning, her daughter could not move her arms.

The girl lay stiff and helpless in bed. The tears ran down her cheeks, and she could not even wipe them away. "Don't let him take me."

The mother gently wiped the tears away. "Of course not."

---

determined   resolved, set
cleaver   large kitchen knife

frantically   very excitedly

The girl rolled her eyes so she could stare at her mother. "How are you going to stop him?"

The mother bit her lip helplessly. "I don't know."

The tears began rolling from the frightened girl's eyes again. "I don't want to marry a ghost."

That gave the determined mother another idea, so she told her daughter to stop. "He wants a bride, but perhaps it doesn't matter who it is."

She went back to the wise old woman, and the old woman suggested a woman who had also died young. Together, they got the consent of her parents and then hurriedly prepared a wedding.

They did everything as if both people had been alive. A red sedan chair was carried to the house of the mother of the dead girl. There, the mother of the sick girl put food and bridal clothes of paper in the chair. Then some young men carried the chair out of the village.

When they first set out, the chair had been light because it only carried food and some paper cutouts. But gradually it grew heavier and heavier until the chair sagged between the poles. The young men had to move slower and said it felt as if they were carrying a real person.

At the stone, the people acted as they would at a real marriage feast. The women even brought hot water and poured it into a basin so the ghost groom could wash his face. When the wedding was over and they were cleaning up, they found the water inside the basin was dirty.

"He must be pleased," the wise old woman said. "He's washed his face like a real person."

When the mother finally returned home, she found her daughter standing in the doorway to greet her.

---

sedan chair   enclosed chair supported on two poles used to carry a person

basin   wash bowl

Laurence Yep has spent most of his life in Northern California where he teaches creative writing at the University of California at Berkeley. He draws on his experiences growing up as a Chinese-American for many of his *fictional* writings.

➤ **Laurence Yep (born 1948)** ◀

AFTER YOU READ

➤ What Do You Think?

Think about the story and discuss it with your classmates and your teacher. Below are some questions to get you started.

1. Using one word, how would you describe the story? Frightening? Funny? Be prepared to read passages that support your description.
2. Describe the girl, the mother, the old woman, or the ghost. Reread everything the character does and says and try to tell what that character is like.
3. What problem are they trying to solve?
4. Does the author build suspense? How?
5. Does the author prepare the reader for a surprise? How?

➤ Try This

Culture Map AM

Although the facts of a story may not be true, the story can reveal things about the culture of the writer or the place where the story is set. The following "Culture Map" lists information that anthropologists, or social scientists who study culture, look at to find out what a culture is like. Which questions can you answer from information in the story or by *inference*—that is, by making an intelligent guess based on information from the story?

CULTURE MAP

Aspects of Culture	Information in "The Ghost's Bride"
Name: What is the culture called?	
Location: Where do the people live?	
Kinship: How are the people related? What are the marriage customs?	
Economics: How do people make a living? What is their idea of success?	
Religion: Does the group practice religion? What are their feelings about spirits, ghosts, death, and life after death?	
Health: How do people in this culture stay healthy? Who are the healers?	
Politics: Who are the decision makers for this group?	

➤ *Learning About Literature*

Creating Suspense

Suspense is a state of uncertainty that may make us feel anxious or excited. We feel suspense when we're not sure what will happen next. Stories often appeal to readers because of their predictability (when readers are able to guess what will happen next) and their unpredictability (when readers can't guess what will happen next). Readers ask questions as they read, and they make guesses about what will happen. If there is no predictability, readers can't make reasonable guesses. If their guesses are always right, readers don't need to finish the story. What questions did you ask as you read the "The Ghost's Bride?" What guesses did you make? Were you usually right? How did the suspense that the author created add to your enjoyment of the story?

You and your classmates may learn more about creating suspense by performing "The Ghost's Bride" as a Reader's Theater. In a Reader's Theater, one person reads a story while other people act out character roles and read the characters' words. Work to build suspense through the expression you use in your reading.

➤ *Writing*

Share some ghost stories in small groups. Make a culture map of the ghost story you or one of your classmates told. Then put the information into *narrative,* or story form, and describe the elements of culture that are revealed in the story.

La Llorona

My grandmother told me a story about a ghost in Mexico. Her name is La Llorona. She walks around at night looking for children.

➤ *Exploring Your Own Experience*

Think-Pair-Share

Authors often create a spooky, eerie feeling of suspense in their stories by choosing words with certain sounds. These sounds might imitate the wind, a knocking on the door, or a mysterious scratching noise.

1. First, think for a few minutes about a spooky story, movie, or frightening personal experience that you have had. What are some of the sounds that come to your mind? Make some notes about what happened and some notes about the spooky sounds that you remember.

2. Next turn to a partner and discuss your ideas about the topic. Write down your partner's spooky sounds.

3. Finally, with your partner, sit with another pair of students. Each person should tell the group the spooky sounds and stories of his or her partner.

➤ *Background*

The poem that follows, "hist whist," may seem different from other poetry you have read. e.e. cummings makes full use of his *poetic license,* which is the freedom to play with and invent language that poets enjoy. The author wrote this poem without a set rhythmic pattern. He invents new words and also uses interesting language patterns to create special effects. Furthermore, he uses capital letters to emphasize certain words or sounds, and he plays with spacing throughout the page to create images. Read or listen to the poem once just to enjoy it. The second time you read it, look for the word patterns that the poet uses.

hist whist

by
e. e. cummings

hist   whist
little ghostthings
tip-toe
twinkle-toe

little twitchy
witches and tingling
goblins
hob-a-nob   hob-a-nob

little hoppy happy
toad in tweeds
tweeds
little itchy mousies

....

twitchy   with quick, uncontrollable
movements
goblins   evil or mischievous spirits,
usually small and ugly
toad   small, frog-like amphibian that
lives on land
tweeds   clothing of rough wool
fabric

The Scream by Edvard Munch, 1893

with scuttling
eyes   rustle and run   and
hidehidehide
whisk

whisk   look out for the old
woman
with the wart on her nose
what she'll do to yer
nobody knows

scuttling   moving quickly, as away
from danger
wart   small hard growth on the skin
yer   you

for she knows the devil   ooch
the devil   ouch
the devil
ach   the great

green
dancing
devil
devil

devil
devil

     wheeEEE

➤ *What Do You Think?*

Think about the poem and discuss it with your classmates and your teacher. Below are some questions to get you started. In your discussion, try to use the text of the poem to support your ideas.

1. What do you think this poem is about?
2. How does the poem make you feel? Do the sounds of the words in the poem affect your feelings?
3. Why do you think cummings signs his name the way he does?
4. In what ways does cummings play with words, punctuation, and line divisions?
5. Find sections you think are playful. Read them to the class and then discuss them.

➤ *Try This*

Word Pairs and Patterns AM

Many pairs or groups of words in this poem are related. For example, "hist" becomes "whist" by changing the initial sound, and "tip-toe" becomes "twinkle-toe" by changing the first word.

1. With a partner, look for as many pairs of related words as you can find.
2. Put each pair on an index card that has been divided into three columns like the one below.
3. In the last column, try to show how the author changed the original word.

First word	Second word	Changes
twitchy	witches	*t* dropped from the beginning of "Twitchy" *y* changed to *es* in "Witches"

➤ Learning About Literature

Free Verse

When poets choose not to use a set rhythmic pattern, they are writing in *free verse*. An example of free verse is "Ode to My Socks" (p. 25). The poet does not use rhyming words or a set rhythm in any part of his poem. This type of verse can make poetry sound more like actual speech.

➤ Writing AM

Write a poem from your own experience using free verse.

1. Write about the last time you were scared, or about some other spooky or suspenseful event.

2. Write two *stanzas*. In the first stanza, use sounds to set a spooky mood. In the second stanza, offer a warning to readers and tell why you are warning them. Try to use some of the spooky language you came up with before reading "hist whist."

3. After you write a first draft, form a group of four students. Look through your first drafts for lines in which you used free verse and poetic license. Then look for other lines where you might use them. If you like your poem, revise it, illustrate it, and try to publish it in some form. For example, you might read it to the class, post it in the classroom, or publish it in the school newspaper.

➤ *Exploring Your Own Experience*

Sharing Your Culture

Many cultures tell stories of people who use special powers for good or evil. Often these stories are *folktales,* tales or legends that are part of the traditions of a culture. Ask your family members to share a folktale they know about people with special powers. Then tell one of their stories to a group of classmates. What elements do the stories have in common? What elements are unique?

➤ *Background*

The following story is one that has been told over and over again in Mexico. It takes place in Córdoba, Mexico, a small city on the Gulf of Mexico near Veracruz. There are also cities called Córdoba in Spain and Argentina.

The Wise Woman of Córdoba

retold by
Francisco Hinojosa

Long ago, in a city called Córdoba, there lived a very beautiful woman. She had lived there as long as anyone could remember. Nobody knew who she was or where she had come from. Even the oldest people in the town could remember her from when they were children. She was called the Wise Woman of Córdoba and it was said that she was in contact with the devil.

In many ways, however, the Wise Woman seemed a good person. She always helped those in difficulty. When young girls were lonely and wanted a husband, they went to the Wise Woman. When young ladies were poor and wanted fine dresses to wear at court, they went to her. When miners were sad because there was no silver in their mines, they, too, went to the Wise Woman. And with her magic powers she fulfilled nonetheless their wishes.

She was so famous that even today, when someone in Mexico asks an impossible favor the answer will be "I'm not the Wise Woman of Córdoba."

Nonetheless, even though she did good deeds, the Wise Woman was clearly a witch. All the young men were in love with her, but she never paid any attention to them. This was one reason why people used to say she was married to the devil. For another, she would appear at the same time to different people, in different places.

---

miners workers who dig up minerals such as coal, iron, gold, or silver from underground

fulfilled granted, made happen
nonetheless anyway

Portrait of Galicia Galant, by Frida Kahlo, 1927

And, what's more, she was often seen flying through the air above the rooftops with bright sparks coming out of her eyes.

Nobody knows exactly why, but one day the authorities took the Wise Woman to Mexico City and put her in prison. Some believe it was because she was a witch, others believe it was because of her money, for when they arrested her they found ten barrels of gold.

In those days witches were burned to death, and one fine day it was announced that the Wise Woman of Córdoba was to be burned. However, no sooner had that news reached the people than suddenly there came other news, even more astonishing, that the witch had escaped.

How could this have happened? She was locked up in prison in Mexico City with guards watching her day and night. Some people thought one thing, others thought another, but what really happened was this.

One day an important judge went to the prison to try to make the Wise Woman confess. He opened the door of her cell, a big room with a high ceiling, and stood amazed at what he saw. On the wall was an enormous ship drawn in charcoal. It was complete in every detail. It had everything a real ship has!

The Wise Woman was sitting in the corner. She looked at him with her strange black eyes and said:

"Sir, what does this ship need to make it perfect?"

The judge, recovering a little, replied:

"Wretched woman! It is you who is far from being perfect. As far as the boat goes, all it needs is someone to sail it."

"Good!" cried the Wise Woman, "Watch me!" and she leapt into the boat and grabbed the tiller!

Then, to the judge's amazement, the sails of the ship filled as if a strong wind were blowing them, and slowly, slowly,

---

sparks   glowing pieces thrown off from a fire

authorities   persons in charge

arrested   taken to jail

barrels   large, cylinder-shaped containers

astonishing   surprising

wretched   pitiful, miserable, mean

tiller   device used to steer a ship

Sunset off coast of Ruegen (Germany) after a stormy day, by J.C.C. Dahl, 1818

the boat began to travel across the wall. As she steered, the Wise Woman laughed at the bewildered judge. The great ship traveled on and began to disappear into the thickness of the wall at the end of the room. Soon it was completely gone, but the mad laughter of the Wise Woman still echoed through the prison.

---

steered   guided in a certain direction
bewildered   lost, confused

echoed   repeated back a sound

➤ *What Do You Think?*

Think about the story and discuss it with your classmates and your teacher. Below are some questions to get you started. In your discussion, be sure to use the text of the story to back up your ideas.

1. What do you think of the beginning of this story? Is it strong and interesting?
2. What hints are given in the story that help you make guesses about what will happen?
3. How would you describe the character of the Wise Woman?
4. Do you think the Wise Woman was bad or good? What evidence can you find in the text to support your opinion?
5. Do you think the Wise Woman was a witch? What evidence can you find in the story to support your answer?
6. Did you predict the ending of the story? Did you like it? Why or why not?
7. In what ways is this story like the ones you and your classmates told one another before reading?

➤ *Try This*

Character Web AM

Use a character web similar to the one below to outline the qualities of the Wise Woman, the main character in the story. You can use a character web in two ways: (1) after reading, to prepare to analyze a character you have read about; (2) before writing, to develop a character for your own story.

1. Put the name of the character in the center of the web.
2. Label each of the four boxes with a descriptive word about the character.
3. Write words in each box that support your description. You may use the Wise Woman's own words and actions, the narrator's words, and your own ideas from your reading of the text.

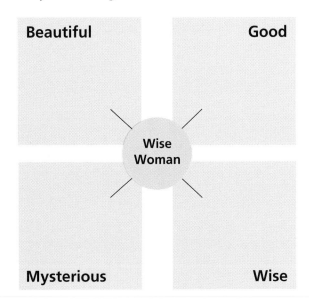

➤ Learning About Literature

The Folktale

Folktales are special kinds of short stories with the following characteristics:

- They originally came from people who could neither read nor write, and they were passed from person to person by the spoken word.
- They often deal with heroes, adventure, magic, or romance.
- There are often many versions of the same folktale.
- Certain magical characters—witches, genies, trolls, leprechauns, and devils—often appear in the stories.

Discuss how this description of a folktale fits "The Wise Woman of Córdoba."

Foreshadowing

Foreshadowing involves using clues to suggest events that have not yet happened. For example, in the first paragraph, the author mentions that "it was said that she [the Wise Woman of Córdoba] was in contact with the devil." Foreshadowing is used to create a feeling of suspense in the reader. What happens later in the text can either fulfill the foreshadowing or surprise the reader. Which happened to you when you read this story?

➤ Writing **AM**

Write down one of the folktales you have heard your family tell. Use the characteristics of folktales to select elements. Use character webs to outline your main characters. If you choose a tale of suspense, try to include foreshadowing.

➤ Exploring Your Own Experience

Two-Column Chart **AM**

Has anyone ever told you an unbelievable story and then insisted that it was true? Share one of these stories with the class. Then discuss what it is about the story that makes you want to believe it, and what it is that makes you doubt it. You might write your ideas on a T-list—a two-column-chart similar to the one below.

Why I want to believe the story.	Why I doubt the story.
My friend said it happened to a friend of his.	I've never seen a ghost.

➤ Background

Some stories are passed on orally from person to person. Some people like to tell ghost stories at night—at family gatherings, on camping trips, or even at school and work. The following two versions of a mysterious story about a hitchhiker were collected by Jan Harold Brunrand. The first version comes from Kunsan, South Korea. The second comes from the state of North Carolina in the United States. You may already have heard a version of this story.

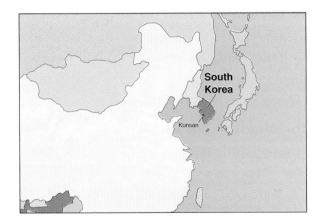

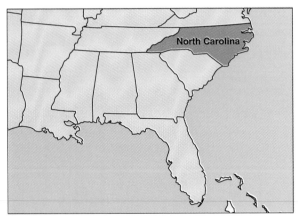

◆

The Hitchhiker

Two versions

Korean Version, told by Haruo Aoki

About midnight a taxi driver of Guntaku Cab Company in Kunsan, Korea, received a telephone call from the municipal crematory asking for a cab. He picked up a young lady of twenty or so in front of the crematory and was told to drive to the hardware store of a Mr. Shimo. When the cab arrived at Mr. Shimo's place on Meiji Street the girl told the driver she did not have the fare and asked him to wait until she could go into the house to get it. Because Mr. Shimo had kept a store at the same location for years and was a respected citizen, the driver waited outside without any misgivings. The girl, however, did not reappear. Finally the driver became impatient and knocked at the closed door. After repeated attempts to arouse somebody in the house, sleepy-looking Mrs. Shimo showed up and asked the driver what he wanted. She seemed to know nothing about the girl's ride. However, after the driver had described the young lady, Mrs. Shimo showed him a picture

----

crematory   place where the bodies of the dead are burned
misgivings   doubts, second thoughts
arouse   awaken

Photo courtesy of Comstock, Inc.

of her daughter on the wall. The daughter had died a few days before and her body had been sent to the same crematory. The driver recognized her immediately and became fatally ill.

....

fatally   deadly

North Carolina Version, told by Douglas J. McMillan

*Mile Post 277,
Blue Ridge Parkway,
North Carolina*

I was riding from Greenville to Winston-Salem, North Carolina and decided to take the old road to Greensboro. It was early dawn and the month was October. I was very drowsy but suddenly woke up when I saw a young girl dressed in a long gown standing on the highway. I stopped and asked her if I could help her. She said that her date had gotten mad when she stopped his advances and had made her get out and walk. I offered to take her home, and she accepted. She didn't say much on the way. When we got there, I got out and came around to open the door for her, but she was gone. I couldn't understand it and went up to the house and rang the bell. When an elderly lady answered, I asked for Mary. "Not again," was all she said. I said, "What?" And she explained that Mary had been killed in a car wreck. I was about the fifth person in eight years that had tried to bring her home. It sure shook me up knowing that I had driven a ghost around.

I just hope that poor girl gets wherever it is she's going.

---

drowsy sleepy

AFTER YOU READ

➤ *What Do You Think?*

Think about the two stories and discuss them with your classmates and your teacher. Below are some questions to get you started. In your discussion, try to use the text of the stories to support your ideas.

1. What are the similarities between the two stories? What are the differences? Why do you think such a story would be told by people in two such distinct cultures?
2. What is it about the way the stories are told that makes you want to believe them? Be as specific as possible.
3. Locate North Carolina, USA, and Kunsan, South Korea, on a map of the world or on a globe.
4. Does the fact that similar stories are told on different sides of the earth make them more or less believable to you?

➤ *Try This*

Comparing and Contrasting Stories Using a Venn Diagram AM

A Venn diagram uses circles to show similarities and differences between topics. Use a Venn diagram like the one below to compare and contrast the two stories.

1. In the left-hand circle, write details and events from the North Carolina version.
2. In the right-hand circle, write details and events from the Korean version.
3. In the intersection, the part where the circles overlap, write details and events that are in both versions.

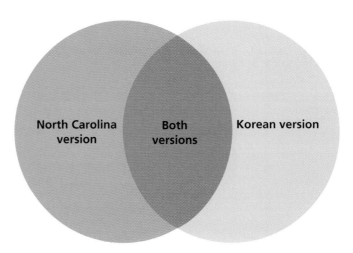

North Carolina version　　Both versions　　Korean version

➤ *Learning About Literature*

Anecdotes AM

An *anecdote* is a brief account of an interesting event in someone's life. The two hitchhiker stories are told in the form of anecdotes, as if they actually happened to the narrator. Anecdotes are often used to make a point, describe a person, or explain an idea, and they can be humorous or serious.

1. Form small groups.
2. Have each person share an anecdote about himself or herself, a friend, or a relative.
3. Discuss what point, idea, or personality trait is revealed.

➤ *Writing*

Anecdotes

Choose one of the following activities:

1. Write an anecdote about someone you know. If you prefer, write a fictional anecdote about someone you know as if it were a true story.
2. Write another version of the hitchhiker story set in still another place or time.

➤ Exploring Your Own Experience

Clustering AM

There are many stories about people who turn into animals or animal monsters. Do you know any of these stories? Have you ever seen a movie about them? Use a cluster map like the one below to create a list of common characteristics of people who turn into animals. What do they look like? How and when do they change? What do they do when they've changed? What do people do to protect themselves from these half-human beasts?

➤ Background

A werewolf, according to legend, is a person who turns into a wolf under the light of the full moon. After the transformation, the werewolf often tries to kill people. Werewolves appear in many old stories, especially in Europe. Tales from other parts of the world tell of people who turn into various other kinds of animals. These animals include tigers in Burma and India, foxes in China and Japan, leopards in western Africa, and jaguars in parts of South America.

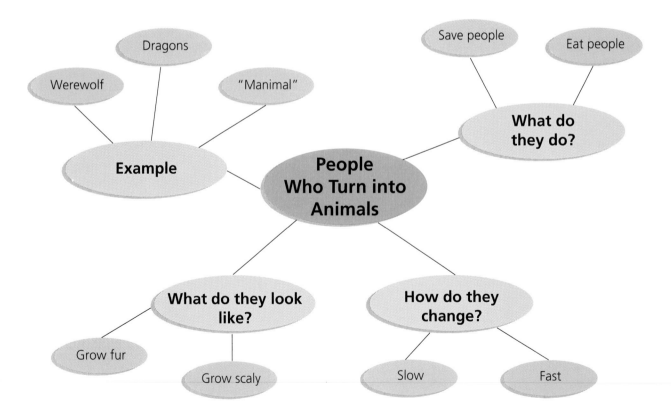

The Wife's Story

by
Ursula K. Le Guin

He was a good husband, a good father. I don't understand it. I don't believe in it. I don't believe that it happened. I saw it happen but it isn't true. It can't be. He was always gentle. If you'd have seen him playing with the children, anybody who saw him with the children would have known that there wasn't any bad in him, not one mean bone. When I first met him he was still living with his mother, over near Spring Lake, and I used to see them together, the mother and the sons, and think that any young fellow that was that nice with his family must be one worth knowing. Then one time when I was walking in the woods I met him by himself coming back from a hunting trip. He hadn't got any game at all, not so much as a field mouse, but he wasn't cast down about it. He was just larking along enjoying the morning air. That's one of the things I first loved about him. He didn't take things hard, he didn't grouch and whine when things didn't go his way. So we got to talking that day. And I guess things moved right along after that, because pretty soon he was over here pretty near all the time. And my sister said—see, my parents had moved out the year before and gone south, leaving us the place—my sister said, kind of teasing but serious, "Well! If

game   animals killed by hunters
cast down   feeling bad
larking   walking light-heartedly or playfully
grouch   complain in an unpleasant manner
whine   complain in a high nasal tone

Photo courtesy of Superstock

he's going to be here every day and half the night, I guess there isn't room for me!" And she moved out—just down the way. We've always been real close, her and me. That's the sort of thing doesn't ever change. I couldn't ever have got through this bad time without my sis.

Well, so he come to live here. And all I can say is, it was the happy year of my life. He was just purely good to me. A hard worker and never lazy, and so big and fine-looking. Everybody looked up to him, you know, young as he was. Lodge Meeting nights, more and more often they had him to lead the singing. He had such a beautiful voice, and he'd lead off strong, and the others following and joining in, high voices and low. It brings the shivers on me now to think of it, hearing it, hearing it, nights when I'd stayed home from meeting when the children was babies—the singing coming up through the trees there, and the moonlight, summer nights, the full moon shining. I'll never hear anything so beautiful. I'll never know a joy like that again.

It was the moon, that's what they say. It's the moon's fault, and the blood. It was in his father's blood. I never knew his father, and now I wonder what become of him. He was from up Whitewater way, and had no kin around here. I always thought he went back there, but now I don't know. There was some talk about him, tales, that come out after what happened to my husband. It's something runs in the blood, they say, and it may never come out, but if it does, it's the change of the moon that does it. Always it happens in the dark of the moon. When everybody's home and asleep. Something comes over the one that's got the curse in his blood, they say, and he gets up because he can't sleep, and goes out into the glaring sun, and goes off all alone—drawn to find those like him.

And it may be so, because my husband would do that. I'd half rouse and say, "Where you going to?" and he'd say, "Oh, hunting, be back this evening," and it wasn't like him, even his voice was different. But I'd be so sleepy, and not wanting to wake the

---

shivers   involuntary shaking caused by cold or fear

curse   evil spell or charm
glaring   brightly shining, so much as to hurt one's eyes
rouse   start to wake up or get up

kids, and he was so good and responsible, it was no call of mine to go asking "Why?" and "Where?" and all like that.

So it happened that way maybe three times or four. He'd come back late, and worn out, and pretty near cross for one so sweet-tempered—not wanting to talk about it. I figured everybody got to bust out now and then, and nagging never helped anything. But it did begin to worry me. Not so much that he went, but that he come back so tired and strange. Even, he smelled strange. It made my hair stand up on end. I could not endure it and I said, "What is that—those smells on you? All over you!" And he said, "I don't know," real short, and made like he was sleeping. But he went down when he thought I wasn't noticing, and washed and washed himself. But those smells stayed in his hair, and in our bed, for days.

And then the awful thing. I don't find it easy to tell about this. I want to cry when I have to bring it to my mind. Our youngest, the little one, my baby, she turned from her father. Just overnight. He come in and she got scared-looking, stiff, with her eyes wide, and then she begun to cry and try to hide behind me. She didn't yet talk plain but she was saying over and over, "Make it go away! Make it go away!"

The look in his eyes, just for one moment, when he heard that. That's what I don't want ever to remember. That's what I can't forget. The look in his eyes looking at his own child.

I said to the child, "Shame on you, what's got into you!"—scolding, but keeping her right up close to me at the same time, because I was frightened too. Frightened to shaking.

He looked away then and said something like, "Guess she just waked up dreaming," and passed it off that way. Or tried to. And so did I. And I got real mad with my baby when she kept on acting crazy scared of her own dad. But she couldn't help it and I couldn't change it.

He kept away that whole day. Because he knew, I guess. It was just beginning dark of the moon.

---

got to bust out   (slang) has to break loose or get away

nagging   complaining about the same thing over and over again

scolding   criticizing, speaking angrily

It was hot and close inside, and dark, and we'd all been asleep some while, when something woke me up. He wasn't there beside me. I heard a little stir in the passage, when I listened. So I got up, because I could bear it no longer. I went out into the passage, and it was light there, hard sunlight coming in from the door. And I saw him standing just outside, in the tall grass by the entrance. His head was hanging. Presently he sat down, like he felt weary, and looked down at his feet. I held still, inside, and watched—I didn't know what for.

And I saw what he saw. I saw the changing. In his feet, it was, first. They got long, each foot got longer, stretching out, the toes stretching out and the foot getting long, and fleshy, and white. And no hair on them.

The hair begun to come away all over his body. It was like his hair fried away in the sunlight and was gone. He was white all over, then, like a worm's skin. And he turned his face. It was changing while I looked. It got flatter and flatter, the mouth flat and wide, and the teeth grinning flat and dull, and the nose just a knob of flesh with nostril holes, and the ears gone, and the eyes gone blue—blue, with white rims around the blue—staring at me out of that flat, soft, white face.

He stood up then on two legs.

I saw him, I had to see him, my own dear love, turned into the hateful one.

I couldn't move, but as I crouched there in the passage staring out into the day I was trembling and shaking with a growl that burst out into a crazy, awful howling. A grief howl and a terror howl and a calling howl. And the others heard it, even sleeping, and woke up.

It stared and peered, that thing my husband had turned into, and shoved its face up to the entrance of our house. I was still bound by mortal fear, but behind me the children had waked up, and the baby was whimpering. The mother anger come into

---

stir movement
weary tired

nostril nose hole
grief deep sadness
terror terrible fear
peered looked
bound held back, restrained
mortal fear fear for one's life
whimpering softly crying

Changeable Wolf/Man by Ha So Da
(Narcisco Abeyta, b. 1918),
Casein on paper

me then, and I snarled and crept forward.

The man thing looked around. It had no gun, like the ones from the man places do. But it picked up a heavy fallen tree branch in its long white foot, and shoved the end of that down into our house, at me. I snapped the end of it in my teeth and started to force my way out, because I knew the man would kill our children if it could. But my sister was already coming. I saw her running at the man with her head low

and her mane high and her eyes yellow as the winter sun. It turned on her and raised up that branch to hit her. But I come out of the doorway, mad with the mother anger, and the others all were coming answering my call, the whole pack gathering, there in that blind glare and heat of the sun at noon.

The man looked round at us and yelled out loud, and brandished the branch it held. Then it broke and ran, heading for the cleared fields and plowlands, down the mountainside. It ran,

---

snarled   made an angry, growling sound bearing teeth

mane   neck hair of an animal

brandished   waved in a threatening manner

on two legs, leaping and weaving, and we followed it.

I was last, because love still bound the anger and the fear in me. I was running when I saw them pull it down. My sister's teeth were in its throat. I got there and it was dead. The others were drawing back from the kill, because of the taste of the blood, and the smell. The younger ones were cowering and some crying, and my sister rubbed her mouth against her forelegs over and over to get rid of the taste. I went up close because I thought if the thing was dead the spell, the curse must be done, and my husband could come back—alive, or even dead, if I could only see him, my true love, in his true form, beautiful. But only the dead man lay there white and bloody. We drew back and back from it, and turned and ran, back up into the hills, back to the woods of the shadows and the twilight and the blessed dark.

....

leaping   jumping

weaving   moving back and forth

cowering   hiding or hanging back in fear

forelegs   front legs of an animal

ABOUT THE AUTHOR

Daughter of an anthropologist and a writer, Ursula Le Guin learned at a young age to respect the cultural diversity of the human family. She began writing stories at age nine. At eleven, she submitted one to *Amazing Stories,* a science fiction magazine. After the story was rejected, she waited ten years before submitting another piece for publication. Le Guin has won many awards for her writing, which includes poetry, fantasy—or what the author calls "made-up myths"—essays, and realistic fiction.

➤ **Ursula K. Le Guin (born 1929)** ◄

AFTER YOU READ

➤ *What Do You Think?*

Think about the story and discuss it with your classmates and your teacher. Below are some questions to get you started. In your discussion, try to use the text of the story to support your ideas.

1. How does Le Guin surprise her readers? At what point did you discover the surprise?

2. After you know the ending, you can find many examples of foreshadowing (p. 81) in the story. Look back over the story for hints that the story was not about a man turning into a wolf, but a wolf turning into a man. Read them aloud to your classmates.

3. Ursula Le Guin uses situational irony (p. 17) in this story. Because we know about werewolves, we expect certain things and overlook others. Can you find details you overlooked? Make a list of key words and phrases—for example the word "whine" (p. 89) might refer to sounds made by a wolf.

4. How does Le Guin describe the sun and the moon in this story? Is she consistent with what we expect of werewolves in her story about a "wereman"?

5. Le Guin is a science fiction and fantasy writer who is well-known for strong characters. Discuss the characters of the wife, the husband, the sister, and the children. Find passages that describe them and their relationships with one another. Describe one of the characters in your own words.

6. Who tells this story? What would the story be like from the point of view of a different character or narrator?

➤ *Try This*

Draw the Setting (AM)

1. Draw two pictures of the home that is the *setting* of this story. Draw a picture of the home as you imagined it *before* you knew who the wife and husband were. Draw a second picture of the home as you imagined it *after* you found out who they were.

2. Get together with a group of four classmates. Discuss your different views about the story. Discuss how you came up with your first drawings. Was it the author's words or your own ideas that made you imagine the first setting?

➤ Learning About Literature

Point of View

Point of view is the relationship of the story-teller to the story. In "The Wife's Story," the point of view is *first-person point of view* because the narrator refers to herself as "I". The narrator is the wife. The story could also be told in the first-person by the husband, the sister, or another character in the story. The North Carolina hitchhiker story you read earlier was also told in the first-person point of view.

The story could also be told from the *limited third-person point of view*. The narrator would not be "I", but the story would be told with the thoughts and ideas of only one character. The Korean hitchhiker story is told with only the information the cab driver would know. It is told from this limited third-person point of view.

A story also can be told in the *omniscient* (all-knowing), or *third-person point of view*. In this telling, the narrator would know the thoughts and feelings of all the characters. "The Ghost's Bride" is told from this point of view.

➤ Writing (AM)

Writing from Another Point of View

Try to retell the beginning or ending of "The Wife's Story" from a point of view that is different from the one Le Guin uses. Your beginning or ending could be told in the first-person by a different person, by a narrator from the omniscient point of view, or by a character from the limited third-person point of view.

In the following example, the beginning of the story is told from the sister's point of view:

> *My sister had a good husband, a good father for her children, we thought. She doesn't understand what happened, but I was always suspicious. He seemed gentle. When I saw him playing with the children, he looked as if there wasn't any bad in him, not one mean bone...*

➤ *Exploring Your Own Experience*

Round Table

Can you think of words you might use to express sadness? In small groups, take turns passing around a sheet of paper, each person adding words that might express this feeling. Use translation and English-English dictionaries and a thesaurus to help you make your list.

➤ *Background*

Edgar Allan Poe is a master at creating a mood. The mood in "The Raven" is melancholy—a deep and mysteriously beautiful sadness. Have you ever experienced such a mood? Poe thought that the word *nevermore*, both for its sound and its meaning, helped him to express this mood.

A Synopsis

A *synopsis* is a brief summary. To help you better understand "The Raven," read the following *synopsis* before reading the poem:

> One dark December night, a poet is feeling tired and sad. He is reading old books to escape his grief over the death of his love, Lenore, when he hears a rapping on his door.
>
> He wonders who is visiting so late, but when he opens the door, he sees no one. He hears only a voice saying, "Lenore." He calls out, "Lenore?" but there is no answer. He hears the knock again, and this time when he opens the door, he sees a raven, who flies in and sits on the head of a statue over the door.
>
> When asked its name, the raven says, "Nevermore." The poet wonders what the raven means. Is it to comfort him? Is it to frighten him?
>
> The poet tells the raven to leave, but the bird refuses and remains forever above the poet's door.

The Raven

by
Edgar Allan Poe

Once upon a midnight dreary,
    while I pondered, weak and weary,
Over many a quaint and curious volume of
forgotten lore,—
While I nodded, nearly napping, suddenly
there came a tapping,
As of some one gently rapping, rapping at
my chamber door.
" 'Tis some visitor," I muttered, "tapping at my chamber door,—
 Only this and nothing more."

Ah, distinctly I remember it was in the bleak
December,
And each separate dying ember wrought its
ghost upon the floor.

---

dreary   dark and dull
pondered   thought about
quaint   strange, pleasantly different, unusual
volume   book
lore   learning
chamber   room
distinctly   clearly
dying ember   coal about to burn out
wrought   shaped, made

Still Life with Books by Henri Matisse, 1890

Eagerly I wished the morrow;—vainly I had sought to borrow
From my books surcease of sorrow,—sorrow
for the lost Lenore—
For the rare and radiant maiden whom the
angels name Lenore—
Nameless *here* for evermore.

And the silken sad uncertain rustling of each
purple curtain
Thrilled me—filled me with fantastic terrors
never felt before;
So that now, to still the beating of my heart, I stood repeating
"Tis some visitor entreating entrance at my chamber door;
Some late visitor entreating entrance at my chamber door.
 This it is and nothing more."

Presently my soul grew stronger; hesitating
then no longer,
"Sir," said I, "or Madam, truly your forgiveness
I implore;
But the fact is I was napping, and so gently
you came rapping,
And so faintly you came tapping, tapping at
my chamber door,

....

morrow   next day, tomorrow
vainly   unsuccessfully
surcease   end
rustling   sound of fabric rubbing together
terrors   terrible fears
entreating   asking, begging
hesitating   pausing, waiting

Northern Raven (Corvus corax) by John James Audubon for his *Birds of America*, 1827-1838

That I scarce was sure I heard you,"— here I
opened wide the door;—
Darkness there and nothing more.

Deep into that darkness peering, long I stood
there wondering, fearing,
Doubting, dreaming dreams no mortal ever
dared to dream before;
But the silence was unbroken, and the stillness
gave no token,
And the only word there spoken
was the whispered word, "Lenore!"
This I whispered, and an echo murmured back
the word, "Lenore!"
Merely this and nothing more.

Back into the chamber turning,
all my soul within me burning,
Soon again I heard a tapping,
somewhat louder than before.
"Surely," said I, "surely that is something
at my window–lattice:
Let me see, then, what thereat is,
and this mystery explore,—
Let my heart be still a moment,
and this mystery explore:
'Tis the wind and nothing more!"

....

scarce   hardly
peering   looking
token   sign
murmured   spoke in soft, rhythmic tone
lattice   crossed strips of metal or wood over an opening

Open here I flung the shutter,
when, with many a flirt and flutter,
In there stepped a stately Raven
of the saintly days of yore.
Not the least obeisance made he, —
not a minute stopped or stayed he,
But, with mien of lord or lady,
perched above my chamber door,—
Perched upon a bust of Pallas
Just above my chamber door,—
Perched, and sat, and nothing more.

Then this ebony bird beguiling
my sad fancy into smiling,
By the grave and stern decorum
of the countenance it wore,
"Though thy crest be shorn and shaven, thou," I said.
"art sure no craven,

---

obeisance   bow

mien   manner

bust   sculpture of head and shoulders

Pallas   Pallas Athene, Greek goddess of wisdom

ebony   black

beguiling   tricking

grave   solemn, serious, not funny

decorum   manner

countenance   the way one holds oneself, the look on one's face

crest   feathers on a bird's head

shorn   cut off

craven   coward

Ghastly, grim, and ancient Raven, wandering from
the Nightly shore.
Tell me what thy lordly name is
on the Night's Plutonian shore!"
Quoth the Raven "Nevermore."

----

ghastly   ghostlike
Plutonian   of the underworld, ruled by Pluto, or Hades, the god of the
lower regions
quoth   said, quoted
* See Appendix A (p. 230) for the remaining text of *The Raven*.

ABOUT THE AUTHOR

Edgar Allan Poe was born in Boston, the son of traveling actors. His mother died when he was still a baby. He led a short and unhappy life, marked by wild living, poverty, and the death, in 1847, of his beloved wife, Virginia. Poe wrote extensively throughout his life, completing one novel and many short stories and poems. Although some writers have criticized his work, others, especially Europeans, consider him one of North America's greatest literary figures.

► **Edgar Allan Poe (1809–1849)** ◄

AFTER YOU READ

➤ *What Do You Think?*

Think about the poem and discuss it with your classmates and your teacher. Below are some questions to get you started. In your discussion, try to use the text of the poem to support your ideas.

1. How would you describe the mood of this poem? What elements of the poem help to create that mood?
2. Describe the setting of the poem in your own words.
3. Many readers enjoy the sounds in Poe's poetry. Listen to the poem again, try to find a line that sounds especially beautiful or interesting to you and read it aloud.

➤ *Try This*

Using Jigsaw Groups **AM**

A *jigsaw* is a puzzle in which all the parts fit together to make a whole. In class, you can divide up "The Raven" as if it were a jigsaw puzzle. Students can work in pairs, and each pair of students can become experts on a small section of the poem. Follow these steps:

1. Work with a partner.
2. With your partner, choose a stanza of "The Raven" to study and *paraphrase*, or retell in your own words.
3. Look up all unfamiliar words in your stanza in an English dictionary and translation dictionary.
4. Rewrite the stanza in your own words.
5. Share your rewritten stanza(s) with the class. Follow the order in which the stanzas appear in the poem.
6. After listening to the paraphrases of all the verses, listen to the poem once again.

➤ Learning About Literature

Assonance

Poets will sometimes repeat a vowel sound in a line of words. This poetic sound device is called *assonance*. An example of assonance in "The Raven" is "...the rare and r<u>a</u>diant m<u>ai</u>den whom the <u>a</u>ngels n<u>a</u>me Lenore" (p. 101). With a partner, try to find two more examples of assonance in "The Raven."

Rhyme Scheme **AM**

As you learned in Unit 1, *rhyme* is the use of identical sounds in some part of a poem, usually at the end of words or lines of verse. For example, *door, lore,* and *more* are rhyming words at the ends of the verses in the first stanza of "The Raven." Rhyme can add to the sound appeal and the meaning of a poem. It can also make a poem easier to remember. The following activities will help you understand the *rhyme scheme,* or the pattern of rhyme, that Poe uses in "The Raven."

1. Look at the last word of each line in the first stanza of the poem. Remember that to describe rhyme schemes, we label each different rhyme with a different letter of the alphabet. When two words rhyme with each other, we give them the same letters.

Rhyme Scheme for First Stanza of "The Raven"	
dreary	a
weary	a
lore	b
tapping	c
door	b
door	b
more	b

2. What is the rhyme scheme of the second stanza? The last stanza?
3. Write down the last word of each line of one of your favorite songs. What is the rhyme scheme of that song?

➤ Writing

Writing About Poetry **AM**

Write a short composition about "The Raven" or another poem of your choice. Include the following:

- What the poem is about
- What mood the poem expresses
- What poetic devices, such as assonance, rhyme, and repetition, the poet uses
- What your response to the poem is
- How the rhyme scheme fits the mood of the poem

Unit Follow-Up

> ## *Making Connections*

Unit Project Ideas

Below are some possible unit projects. If you like, think up a project of your own. You can use some of the tools and techniques you have seen in this unit to help you plan and complete your project.

1. Journal of the Weird. Keep a class journal of strange and scary anecdotes. Whenever someone has an unusual story to tell, someone records the story in a special notebook. The stories and ideas from this notebook can be expanded or revised for other unit projects.

2. Class Book of Suspense. Create a class book of suspenseful writings and illustrations. Include poetry, ghost stories, and your own scary anecdotes. (Optional: use word processing and/or publishing software to produce your book).

3. Family Folktales. Collect and write down suspenseful or eerie family anecdotes.

4. Analyzing Rhyme Scheme. Pick a song or poem that rhymes. Analyze the rhyme scheme. Write about how the rhyme "works." How does it add to the quality of the song or poem?

5. Holiday Customs. Write a report about the customs of special holidays such as Halloween or the Mexican holiday *Día de los Muertos* (Day of the Dead). Write from your own experience or interview people who celebrate that holiday. Illustrate your report with photos, pictures from magazines, or your own drawings.

6. Story Telling. Plan a class "campfire" story telling session. Each person brings to class a spooky story to share. Turn out the lights, gather around a shaded lamp on the floor, and tell stories. (Optional: use data-base software to organize information about holidays celebrated in your classmates' cultures).

7. Oral Interpretation. Perform an oral reading or recitation of "hist whist" or "The Raven." You may wish to perform in a group and have each person memorize part of the poem.

8. Reader's Theater. Perform "The Ghost's Bride," "The Wise Woman of Córdoba," or another suspenseful story as a Reader's Theater.

Further Reading

Below are some books related to this unit that you might enjoy.

• *The Trouble with Lemons,* by Daniel Hayes. Ballantine Books, 1992. In this suspenseful novel, a teenage boy, Tyler, and his friend Lymie learn about themselves and how they fit into their very different families while they solve a murder mystery. Tyler realizes that he is not a "lemon," even if he isn't perfect.

• *Mexico: The Day of the Dead,* compiled by Chloe Sayer. Shambhala Redstone Editions, 1993. A multimedia anthology which includes poetry, articles, cartoons, photographs, and explanations about Mexico's Day of the Dead celebration.

• *Scary Stories to Tell in the Dark,* by Alvin Schwartz. Harper/Collins Publishers, 1981 (Volume 1), 1984 (Volume 2), and 1991 (Volume 3). Stories and folklore from around the world about witches, zombies, and other creatures.

• *Speak to the Rain,* by Helen K. Passey. Atheneum, 1991. A young girl agrees to forfeit her life so that the spirits of a lost Northwest Native-American tribe can be led from their hundred year imprisonment.

• *The Rainbow People,* by Laurence Yep. Harper and Row Publishers, 1989. A collection of whimsical and mysterious tales told by Chinese-Americans.

• *The Vanishing Hitchhiker: American Urban Legends and their Meanings,* edited by Jan H. Brunvand. W.W. Norton and Co, Inc., 1981. A collection of various versions of a story in which a ghost returning in human form is offered a ride late at night.

• *Werewolves: A Collection of Original Stories,* edited by Jane Yolen and Martin Greenberg. Harper and Row, 1990. This is a collection of fifteen werewolf stories by well-known fantasy writers.

Chez le Père Lathuille by Édouard Manet, 1879

UNIT 3

Love

Love, the theme of this third unit, is a universal human experience. You will read about different kinds of love: love of families, young love, and love in marriage. The selections come from many genres—a letter, poems, plays, and stories—and look at love from the viewpoints of several cultures.

➤ Exploring Your Own Experience

Concentric Circles

Where do you live? Can you describe where you live as a series of places, one inside the other, each smaller and more specific? Use the chart of concentric circles—smaller circles inside larger ones—to help you.

1. Work with a partner.
2. Draw a diagram of concentric circles like the one shown below. Try to name all the inner circles.
3. When you finish, compare your names for the circles with those of another pair of students.
4. Try to name something or someone important to you in each of these places.

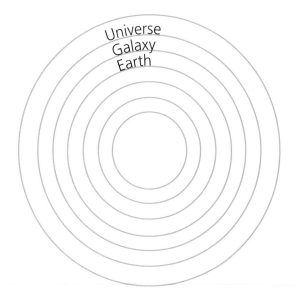

➤ Background

The *anonymous,* or unknown, author of the poem that follows is from India. Sometimes authors' names are forgotten, but the authors are still remembered through their words.

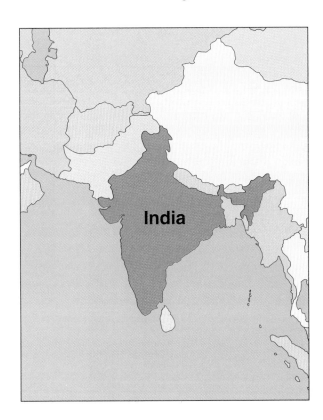

Although I Conquer
All the Earth

Anonymous, Ancient India

Although I conquer all the earth,
Yet for me there is only one city.
In that city there is for me only one house;
And in that house, one room only;
And in that room, a bed.
And one woman sleeps there,
The shining joy and jewel of all my kingdom.

Desvarati Ragini, page
from a dispersed Ragamala
Manuscript 1605-6, India

➤ *What Do You Think?*

Think about the poem and discuss your ideas with classmates and your teacher. Below are some other ideas and questions to talk about. Whenever possible, refer to the text of the poem to support your ideas.

1. Who do you imagine the *speaker* of the poem is? On what words in the poem can you base your ideas?

2. What places and things are important to the speaker? What is the *most* important?

3. Where does the poem begin? Where does it end?

4. Are any words, phrases, or patterns repeated?

5. Can you fit the pattern of the poem into concentric circles like those that you used in *Exploring Your Own Experience* on page 112?

➤ *Learning about Literature*

Imagery AM

Reading poetry, like writing poetry, is a creative activity in which you use your imagination. That is one reason why reading poetry is so satisfying. Poets use *imagery* to help their readers create images or pictures in their minds. What were some of the pictures you imagined when you read or listened to this poem?

Parallelism

Poets and other writers often use *parallelism,* or parallel construction, to create patterns in their writing. In mathematics, parallel lines extend in the same direction. In writing, parallel structures repeat a pattern either exactly or with some variation.

In "Although I Conquer All the Earth," the poet repeats, with variations, the idea that there is only one important item in each place: one earth, one city, one house, one room, one bed, one woman. The word pattern is also repeated. Notice that every line ends with the name of a place that is important to the poet—earth, city, and so on. In each new line, the writer seems to look at his love through a telescope using a stronger lens, starting far away and gradually moving closer and closer.

➤ Try This

Using Parallel Structures AM

1. Describe someone or something important to you by telling where it is. Use the parallel structure used in the poem, "Although I Conquer All the Earth." You can start far away and come closer, as the poet does, or you may choose to start up close and move farther away with each line.

2. Write your ideas on a "Concentric Circles" chart like the one on page 112.

➤ Writing

Using the ideas on your "Concentric Circles" chart, write in your journal a first draft of a poem about someone or something that is important to you. You may want to read your draft to a classmate and ask him or her to respond to your poem.

➤ Exploring Your Own Experience

Think-Pair-Share AM

1. Think for a few minutes about the following questions:
   - What do you think a man's role in a marriage is? What do you think a woman's role in a marriage is?
   - Are there some roles that only men typically play and others that only women typically play?
   - Are there some roles that both play?
   - Do you know any couples with roles that are not typical?
2. Discuss your ideas with a classmate. Listen carefully to your partner's ideas.
3. With your partner, join another pair of students. Each person in your group should tell what his or her partner's ideas are.
4. When you finish your discussion, each group can write one or more ideas on a class chart that summarizes the answers to the questions.

➤ Background

The events in the following *narrative,* or story, actually took place in the central highlands of Vietnam in the early twentieth century.

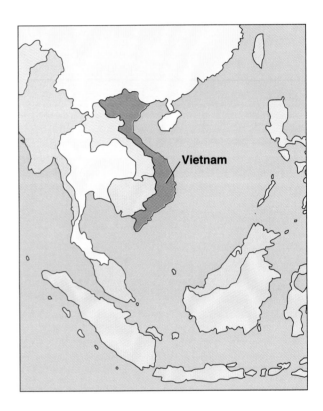

Karate

**From *The Land I Lost*
by Huynh Quang Nhuong**

My grandmother had married a man whom she loved with all her heart, but who was totally different from her. My grandfather was very shy, never laughed loudly, and always spoke very softly. And physically he was not as strong as my grandmother. But he excused his lack of physical strength by saying that he was a "scholar."

About three months after their marriage, my grandparents were in a restaurant and a rascal began to insult my grandfather because he looked weak and had a pretty wife. At first he just made insulting remarks, such as, "Hey! Wet chicken! This is no place for a weakling!"

My grandfather wanted to leave the restaurant even though he and my grandmother had not yet finished their meal. But my grandmother pulled his shirt sleeve and signaled him to remain seated. She continued to eat and looked as if nothing had happened.

Tired of yelling insults without any result, the rascal got up from his table, moved over to my grandparents' table, and grabbed my grandfather's chopsticks. My grandmother immediately wrested the chopsticks from him and struck the rascal

rascal   scoundral, troublemaker
wrested   pulled away, usually after a struggle

Night view of Saruwaka-machi by Utagawa Hiroshige (1797-1858)

on his cheekbone with her elbow. The blow was so quick and powerful that he lost his balance and fell on the floor. Instead of finishing him off, as any street fighter would do, my grandmother let the rascal recover from the blow. But as soon as he got up again, he kicked over the table between him and my grandmother, making food and drink fly all over the place. Before he could do anything else, my grandmother kicked him on the chin. The kick was so swift that my grandfather didn't even see it. He only heard a heavy thud, and then saw the rascal tumble backward and collapse on the ground.

All the onlookers were surprised and delighted, especially the owner of the restaurant. Apparently the rascal, one of the best karate fighters of our area, came to his restaurant every day and left without paying for his food or drink, but the owner was too afraid to confront him.

While the rascal's friends tried to revive him, everyone else surrounded my grandmother and asked her who had taught her karate. She said, "Who else? My husband!"

After the fight at the restaurant people assumed that my grandfather knew karate very well but refused to use it for fear of killing someone. In reality, my grandmother had received special training in karate from my great-great uncle from the time she was eight years old.

---

revive   wake up, bring back to consciousness
assumed   something that is believed but not proven

View of Nihonbashi Tori I-chome by Utagawa Hiroshige (1797-1858)

Anyway, after that incident, my grandfather never had to worry again. Any time he had some business downtown, people treated him very well. And whenever anyone happened to bump into him on the street, they bowed to my grandfather in a very respectful way.

---

incident happening, event

ABOUT THE AUTHOR

Huynh Quang Nhuong was born in Mytho, in the central highlands of Vietnam. He was injured while fighting for the South Vietnamese army, and in 1969 he came to the United States for medical treatment. Although he is permanently paralyzed by his injury, Mr. Huynh has received a bachelor's and a master's degrees in French and Comparative Literature. His book, *The Land I Lost,* is the story of his boyhood in Vietnam.

➤ **Huynh Quang Nhuong (born 1946)** ◄

AFTER YOU READ

➤ *What Do You Think?*

Think about the story and discuss it with your classmates and your teacher. Below are some questions to get you started. In your discussion, be sure to use the text of the story to support your ideas.

1. How does the author begin this story? Did it get your attention? Did you want to read more? What questions were in your mind?

2. What events or characterizations in the story are not the way you expect them to be? Read passages aloud to support your examples.

3. Did you find any parts of the story funny? What do you think the author did to make those parts humorous?

4. How do you think this story relates to the unit theme of love? In what ways do the characters show love for each other?

5. Compare the roles of the man and the woman in this story to the ideas you summarized on the class chart in the "Think-Pair-Share" exercise. Has the story changed your ideas of typical roles at all?

➤ *Try This*

Story Mapping AM

A *story map* can be used in several ways. It can provide an outline of a story before you read it, help you analyze the plot of a story after you read it, or help you outline a story as you prepare to write.

Analyze the plot of "Karate" by filling in the following story map.

Story Map of "Karate"	
Story Elements:	
Characters:	
Setting:	
Initial Event:	
Reaction:	
Goal-setting:	
Attempts to Reach Goal:	
Outcome:	
Resolution:	

Learning About Literature

Leads and Conclusions

Good writers pay close attention to the *lead*, how the writing begins, and the *conclusion*, how the writing ends. The lead sets the tone of the piece and catches the reader's interest. The conclusion reveals the story's outcome and leaves a final impression with the reader.

1. Look back at the lead and conclusion of "Karate" and discuss your first and final impressions.
2. Compare the lead and conclusion of the story with the leads and conclusions of other stories you have read. Which leads and conclusions do you think are best? Why?

Writing

1. Use a story map to outline an interesting incident in your life or a family story that you have heard.
2. Write a lead sentence for the story, paying close attention to how you will set the tone and get the reader's attention.
3. Write a concluding sentence that reveals the resolution of the story and leaves a strong final impression with the reader.
4. Share your story outline, lead, and conclusion with your writing response group.
5. Try to offer encouraging comments to other group members.
6. Use your classmates' ideas and comments to complete, revise, and edit your narrative.
7. Edit your piece for publication.

➤ Exploring Your Own Experience

How Do You Say Goodbye to Your Loved Ones? AM

In English, people say goodbye to one another in many ways. They say *goodbye* (which comes from "God be with you"), *so long,* or *see you later,* to name a few. With two classmates, make a list of as many ways to say goodbye as you can think of, in as many languages as you know. Include the English meanings of these words or phrases, if you can figure them out. Each group should list its ideas on a chart like the one below and then explain and demonstrate at least one idea to the class.

How Do You Say Goodbye?		
How Do You Say Goodbye?	Language:	English Meaning:
goodbye	English	God be with you
aloha	Hawaiian	hello and goodbye
ciao	Italian	hello or so long
adiós	Spanish	to God

➤ Background

Do you find it difficult to say goodbye? Does it seem harder or easier in other languages or cultures? Are there languages with no word for goodbye? These are some of the questions addressed in the following poem, written by an Athabaskan poet from Alaska.

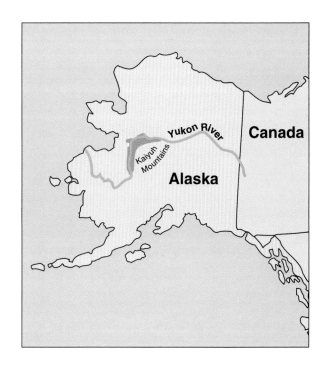

There Is No Word for Goodbye

by
Mary TallMountain

Sokoya, I said, looking through
    the net of wrinkles into
    wise black pools
    of her eyes.

What do you say in Athabaskan
    when you leave each other?
    What is the word
    for goodbye?

A shade of feeling rippled
    the wind-tanned skin.
    Ah, nothing, she said,
    watching the river flash.

Sokoya aunt, mother's sister
Athabaskan a group of North American
Indians

Totem Pole, Sitka National Historic Park, Sitka, Alaska

She looked at me close.
>We just say, Tlaa. That means,
>See you.
>We never leave each other.
>When does your mouth
>say goodbye to your heart?

She touched me light
>as a bluebell.
>You forget when you leave us;
>you're so small then.
>We don't use that word.

We always think you're coming back,
>but if you don't,
>we'll see you some place else.
>You understand.
>There is no word for goodbye.

ABOUT THE AUTHOR

Mary TallMountain, born Mary Demonski, comes from the interior of Alaska. The mountainous terrain of the Kaiyuh mountain range along Alaska's Yukon River has greatly influenced her work. The daughter of Athabaskan-Russian and Scotch-Irish parents, she now lives near San Francisco.

➤ **Mary TallMountain (born 1917)** ◄

AFTER YOU READ

➤ *What Do You Think?*

Think about the poem and discuss it with your classmates and your teacher. Below are some questions to get you started. In your discussion, try to use the text of the poem to support your ideas.

1. What are the ways to say goodbye in Athabaskan? How do they compare with the ways on the chart that you made?
2. Why do so many ways of saying goodbye seem indirect?
3. Is saying goodbye hard for you to do?
4. Do you think it's harder to say goodbye in some cultures than in others? Why?
5. Why do you think the poet wrote about this subject?
6. What do you think the poet means when she writes, "When does your mouth say goodbye to your heart?"

➤ *Try This*

Marking the Poem AM

For this activity you will need a copy of the poem "There Is No Word for Goodbye" to write on and three different colored pens or highlighters. If you don't have a copy to write on, use self-stick notes or bookmarks. If you don't have three different colored pens or highlighters, mark the words in three different ways, for example, by underlining, circling, or marking with a star.

1. Read the poem once. In the first color, highlight any words that confuse or surprise you. After reading the entire poem check the meaning of new words with your classmates, with your teacher, or in a dictionary.
2. Read the poem a second time. In the second color, highlight words that show a shift or change of ideas in the poem.
3. Read the poem two more times with a partner. As your partner reads the poem aloud to you, highlight the words he or she stresses. Then reverse roles for another reading.
4. Compare your highlighted poem with your partner's. Discuss differences and similarities.
5. Share what you learned with the class.

➤ Learning About Literature

Imagery AM

In "There Is No Word for Goodbye," the poet uses many images from nature to share the feelings and values of the Athabaskans. For example, she describes the old woman's eyes as "wise black pools" surrounded by a "net of wrinkles."

1. How do you think the poet feels about the old woman?
2. Can you find other examples of imagery from nature in the poem?
3. Can you find examples of similes or metaphors in the poem?
4. What do these images tell you about the Athabaskan culture?

➤ Writing AM

Visit a beautiful outdoor spot—perhaps a neighborhood park, a garden, or your own backyard. While you are there, write a *description* of that place. Try to be aware of your senses—describe what you see, hear, feel, smell, or taste. Do images in nature have multiple meanings in your writing?

➤ *Exploring Your Own Experience*

Two-Column Chart **AM**

Working in groups of about four, make a two-column chart about love like the one below. At the top of the first column of your chart, write, "Love is." At the top of the second column of your chart, write, "Love is not." Pass the chart around the group. Each person should add one idea to each column. Keep passing the chart around until you run out of ideas. You can help each other at any time. When all of the groups are finished, share your ideas with the whole class. Summarize what love means to your class.

➤ *Background*

Carl Sandburg's poetry can sometimes seem a little strange or mysterious to the reader. You may find you don't always agree with others about what the poem means. Sandburg writes his thoughts the same way we think our own thoughts—one image flows into another. Like e. e. cummings, he uses *free verse;* that is, he writes without rhyme and with no fixed rhythms.

Love Is, Love Is Not

Love is	Love is not
giving	being selfish
dancing all night	playing Trivial Pursuit
helping one another	a one-way street

Solo for Saturday Night Guitar

by
Carl Sandburg

Time was. Time is. Time shall be.
Man invented time to be used.
Love was. Love is. Love shall be.
Yet man never invented love
Nor is love to be used like time.
A clock wears numbers one to twelve
And you look and read its face
And tell the time pre-cise-ly ex-act-ly.
Yet who reads the face of love?
Who tells love numbers pre-cise-ly ex-act-ly?
Holding love in a tight hold for keeps,
Fastening love down and saying
"It's here now and here for always."
You don't do this offhand, careless-like.

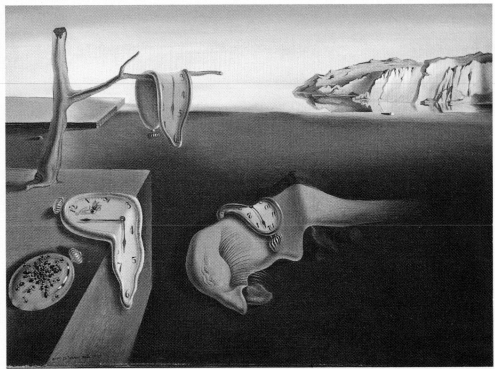

The Persistence of Memory by Salvador Dali, 1931

Love costs. Love is not so easy
Nor is the shimmering of star dust
Nor the smooth flow of new blossoms
Nor the drag of a heavy hungering for someone.
    Love is a white horse you ride
    or wheels and hammers leaving you lonely
    or a rock in the moonlight for rest
    or a sea where phantom ships cross always
    or a tall shadow always whispering
    or a circle of spray and prisms—

....

shimmering   shining, sparkling like water at night

phantom   ghost

prisms   pieces of glass shaped to turn light into rainbows

maybe a rainbow round your shoulder.
 Heavy heavy is love to carry
 and light as one rose petal,
 light as a bubble, a blossom,
 a remembering bar of music
 or a finger or a wisp of hair
 never forgotten.

....

petal part of a flower blossom
wisp a small piece or strand

ABOUT THE AUTHOR

Carl Sandburg, the son of a black-smith, earned his own living from the age of thirteen. His love of the United States is evident in his many poems and also in his Pulitzer Prize-winning, six-volume *biography* of Abraham Lincoln. The famous words of Abraham Lincoln himself can actually be used to describe Sandburg. He was, "of the people, by the people, and for the people."

➤ **Carl Sandburg (1878–1967)** ◄

AFTER YOU READ

➤ *What Do You Think?*

Think about the poem and discuss it with your classmates and your teacher. Below are some questions to get you started. In your discussion, try to use the text of the poem to support your ideas.

1. In the first part of the poem, Sandburg compares time and love. Why do you think he chose this comparison? How does he compare the two concepts? How would you make this comparison?

2. In the second part of the poem, Sandburg describes what he thinks love is and what he thinks love is not. How do his ideas compare with the ideas that you listed in your two-column chart before reading the poem?

3. What do the things that love is have in common with one another? What do the things that love is not have in common with one another? What new insights do you get from Sandburg's descriptions?

4. The poet says, "Heavy heavy is love to carry/and light as one rose petal." In what ways can love be both heavy and light at the same time?

5. The poet writes, "Love is a white horse you ride." Do you like this image? What does it tell you about love? Do you agree with this view of love?

6. Can you find connections between the title and the poem? Find the lines of the poem that support your ideas. Read those lines aloud to the class.

➤ *Learning About Literature*

Metaphor

In a *metaphor*, a poet describes something by calling it something else. For example, Sandburg writes, "Love is a sea where phantom ships cross always." In this way, he compares love to a sea. Notice that the words "like" and "as" are not used in a metaphor.

1. Reread the poem to a classmate.
2. Find as many metaphors as you can from "Solo for Saturday Night Guitar."
3. Together, choose your favorite metaphor and explain it to the class.

➤ *Try This*

Love Is..., Love Is Not... **AM**

Write some metaphors using Sandburg's pattern: Love is.../Love is not... Use a two-column chart like the one you made before you read the poem to organize your ideas. You might like to include paintings or drawings to illustrate your metaphors.

➤ *Writing* AM

1. Revise some of your metaphors into a poem. You might choose to compare love to another concept, as Sandburg compared it to time.
2. Meet with a writing-response group of about four classmates. Take turns reading your poems aloud to the group.
3. After each person reads, offer some encouragement and feedback on the poem. Use a poetry-response form like the one below to help you remember ideas for your responses.
4. After you listen to your classmates' responses and discuss them, you may wish to use these ideas to revise and edit your poem for publication.

Poetry Response Form

What did you like about this poem?

_____

_____

_____

What did you think about:
- the words?

_____

_____

_____

- the subject?

_____

_____

_____

- its mysteriousness?

_____

_____

_____

- the way the words appear on the page?

_____

_____

- the way the words sound?

_____

_____

_____

What mood does the poem put you in?

_____

_____

What does the poem remind you of?

_____

_____

_____

What does the poem make you think about?

_____

_____

_____

How does the poem make you feel?

_____

_____

_____

➤ Exploring Your Own Experience

Do a Quickwrite

What would you say to someone you love if you thought you might never see him or her again? Think about your response for a few minutes. Then do a *quickwrite* to expand on your ideas.

A quickwrite is an activity to help you to write with ease. Here are some suggestions for your quickwrite and follow-up activities:

1. Write without stopping for five to ten minutes about what you would say to your loved one.
2. Write your thoughts as they come to you. You don't even have to use sentences; just jot down a few words or phrases to help you remember each idea.
3. When you finish your quickwrite, read it aloud to a classmate.
4 Use the ideas that come up in your discussion to revise your piece later.
5. With your partner, discuss your different ways of responding.

➤ Background

From 1861 to 1865, the United States was torn apart by a civil war between the northern states and the southern states. A major battle of this war, Manassas, also known as the First Battle of Bull Run, took place in the state of Virginia on July 21, 1861. A week before Manassas, Major Sullivan Ballou of the Second Rhode Island Volunteers wrote home to his wife in Smithfield, Rhode Island.

The Sullivan Ballou Love Letter

by
Sullivan Ballou

July 14, 1861
Camp Clark, Washington

My very dear Sarah:
The indications are very strong that we shall move in a few days—perhaps tomorrow. Lest I should not be able to write again, I feel impelled to write a few lines that may fall under your eye when I shall be no more …

I have no misgivings about, or lack of confidence in the cause in which I am engaged, and my courage does not halt or falter. I know how strongly American Civilization now leans on the triumph of the Government, and how great a debt we owe to those who went before us through the blood

....

indications   signs, clues
lest   in case, should
feel impelled   feel the need
misgivings   second thoughts, regrets
triumph   success, victory

Trooper Meditating Beside a Grave by Winslow Homer, 1865

and sufferings of the Revolution. And I am willing—perfectly willing—to lay down all my joys in this life, to help maintain this Government, and to pay that debt...

Sarah my love for you is deathless, it seems to bind me with mighty cables that nothing but Omnipotence could break; and yet my love of Country comes over me like a strong wind and bears me unresistably on with all these chains to the battle field.

The memories of the blissful moments I have spent with you come creeping over me, and I feel most gratified to God and to you that I have enjoyed them so long. And hard it is for me to give them up and burn to ashes the hopes of future years, when, God willing, we might still have lived and loved together, and seen our sons grown up to honorable manhood, around us. I have, I know, but few and small claims upon Divine Providence, but something whispers to me—perhaps it is the wafted prayer of my little Edgar, that I shall return to my loved ones unharmed. If I do not my dear Sarah, never forget how much I love you, and when my last breath escapes me on the battle field, it will whisper your name. Forgive my many faults, and the many pains I have caused you. How thoughtless and foolish I have often times been! How gladly would I wash out with my tears every little spot upon your happiness...

....

cables strong wires
Omnipotence the all-powerful God
blissful very happy
Divine Providence gifts or goodness of God
wafted floating on air

A Civil War Soldier and His Wife, photo courtesy of the Atlanta History Center

But, O Sarah! if the dead can come back to this earth and flit unseen around those they loved, I shall always be near you; in the gladdest days and in the darkest nights...*always, always,* and if there be a soft breeze upon your cheek, it shall be my breath, as the cool air fans your throbbing temple, it shall be my spirit passing by. Sarah do not mourn me dead; think I am gone and wait for thee, for we shall meet again…

---

flit   fly lightly and quickly, like a butterfly

breeze   gentle wind

throbbing   pulsating, like a heartbeat

temple   the side of the face next to the eye

mourn   feel sorrow or sadness for someone who has died

ABOUT THE AUTHOR

Major Sullivan Ballou was killed at the First Battle of Bull Run, where 3,000 Northern soldiers and 2,000 Southern soldiers lost their lives. Almost 620,000 soldiers died during the Civil War. Nearly as many U.S. soldiers died in the Civil War as have died in all other U.S. wars combined, from the American Revolution to the Vietnam War.

➤ **Major Sullivan Ballou** ◄

AFTER YOU READ

➤ *What Do You Think?*

Think about the letter and discuss it with your classmates and your teacher. Below are some questions to get you started. Try to use the text of the letter to support your ideas.

1. Why do you think Sullivan Ballou decided to write this letter?
2. How does Sullivan Ballou feel about the cause he is fighting for?
3. How does he feel about his wife and family?
4. Find the words in the letter that you think express the conflict, or inner struggle, that Ballou feels because of his two commitments. Have you ever experienced such a conflict yourself? Have you heard or read about this kind of conflict in others?
5. Do you think Ballou's words comforted his wife after she found out that he had died? Why or why not?

➤ *Try This*

Charting Words AM

Sullivan Ballou writes powerfully about two things he loves. Look for ideas and phrases that express his love for his country and his love for his family. Write them on a chart like the one below.

Sullivan Ballou's Two Loves	
Country	*Family*

➤ Learning About Literature

Voice

In this short letter, the reader comes to know the author and his family personally. The *voice* of the author is very strong. This powerful voice is created by use of the first person, by the expression of deep feelings, by details of family memories, and by the repeated use of Sarah's name. Can you find examples of each of these? Can you give other reasons the author's voice is so powerful in this letter?

Conflict AM

Another element that lends power to the writing in this letter is *conflict*. Conflict can be described as a struggle between things or ideas that oppose or seem to fight against one another. For example, Ballou feels a conflict between his duty to his country and his duty to his family. Look for details in which Ballou describes this conflict in the letter. Look for other examples of conflict in the letter and add them to the chart below.

Conflicts in Ballou's Letter	
Duty to country	*Duty to family*

AFTER YOU READ

Contrast **AM**

Through *contrast,* an author describes objects or ideas by comparing them with something quite different. For example, Ballou contrasts the strong wind that takes men to war with the soft breeze of his own breath on his wife's cheek. Can you find other examples of the use of contrast in the letter? Use another T-List, or two-column chart, to write down the contrasts in the letter.

➤ *Writing*

Writing a Letter **AM**

Use the ideas from the quickwrite you did at the beginning of this selection and the ideas that you learned from the reading, discussion, and activities to write your own letter. Here are two possible topics:

1. Write a personal letter to a loved one.

Contrast in Sullivan Ballou's Letter	
Possibility of death by war	*Love that is deathless*
Nature as a strong wind taking men to war	*Nature as a soft breeze—a husband's breath upon his wife's cheek*

2. Write an historical love letter from someone who is about to be separated from a
loved one by an historical event. You
might choose a time or topic from your
social studies or history classes. Do some
background reading about the historical
event so that the historical facts will be
accurate and the writing vivid.

In your love letter, you can follow this standard format. For the body of the letter, use a
new paragraph for each idea. For the closing
of the letter use a closing phrase such as *Love,*
or *Yours truly.* See the sample format below.

_____
(date)

_____

_____
(address of writer)

Dear _____ ,
(salutation)

(body) _____

_____

_____

_____

_____

_____
(closing)

_____
(signature of writer)

➤ Exploring Your Own Experience

Ranking Ladder (AM)

This *ranking ladder* activity and the following *Sharing Your Ideas* activity will help to guide you through the next two reading selections. The two plays have similar story lines. Both scenes take place on a balcony. In both scenes, two young lovers whose families are on opposite sides of a serious conflict declare their love for each other. To make a ranking ladder:

1. Try to think of qualities or characteristics that you think a person should look for in a boyfriend or a girlfriend.
2. Write down all the ideas you can think of.
3. Now rank all of those ideas on a ranking ladder, similar to the one below. Put the most important ideas at the top, the least important ideas at the bottom, and the other ideas where they fit in between.

Ranking Ladder

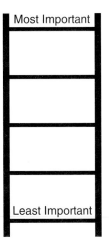

Most Important

Least Important

Sharing Your Ideas

With a partner, try to answer the following questions. Use your ranking ladder to help you. Then, with your partner, join another pair of students. Take turns talking, and allow each person to tell the group what his or her partner's answers were. Don't reject anyone's ideas or answers, even if they sound a bit crazy.

1. What would your family say if you wanted to date someone they disliked or didn't feel comfortable with—perhaps someone with a different background?
2. What would your family say if you wanted to date someone outside your cultural group?
3. Do you think there can be advantages to dating or marrying someone from a very different background or even a different culture? Are there disadvantages?

➤ Background

West Side Story is about two young lovers, Tony and Maria. Tony is the son of Polish immigrants, and Maria is the daughter of Puerto Rican immigrants. Tony's friends and Maria's brother, Bernardo, are members of opposing street gangs, the Jets and the Sharks. Tony and Maria fall in love the moment they see each other at a dance in the school gym. Later that night, Tony visits Maria on the fire escape outside her room.

Balcony Scene from West Side Story

by
Leonard Bernstein, Arthur Laurents, and Steven Sondheim

(Tony *sings)*
Maria, Maria…
Maria.
Ssh!
Tony.
Maria!
Maria.
Quiet!
Tony.
Come down.
Maria.
No.
Tony.
Maria…
Maria.
Please. If Bernardo —
Tony.
He's at the dance. Come down.
Maria.
He will soon bring Anita home.
Tony.
Just for a minute.
Maria.
(Smiles) A minute is not enough.

Photo courtesy of Comstock, Inc.

Tony.

(Smiles) For an hour, then.

Maria.

I cannot.

Tony.

Forever!

Maria.

Ssh!

Tony.

Then I'm coming up.

Woman's Voice.

(From the offstage apartment) Maria!

Maria.

Momentito, Mama...

Tony.

(Climbing up) Maria, Maria—

Maria.

Cállate! (Reaching her hand out to stop him) Ssh!

Tony.

(Grabbing her hand) Ssh!

Maria.

It is dangerous.

Tony.

I'm *not* "one of them."

Maria.

You are; but to me, you are not. Just as I am one of them— *(She gestures toward the apartment.)*

Tony.

To me, you are all the—*(She covers his mouth with her hand.)*

---

momentito *(Spanish)* just a minute

cállate *(Spanish)* be quiet

gestures points

Man's Voice.

(From the unseen apartment) Maruca!

Maria.

Sí ya vengo, Papa.

Tony.

Maruca?

Maria.

His pet name for me.

Tony.

I like him. He will like me.

Maria.

No. He is like Bernardo: afraid. *(Suddenly laughing)* Imagine being afraid of you!

Tony.

You see?

Maria.

(Touching his face) I see you.

Tony.

See only me.

(Maria *sings)*

Only you , you're the only thing I'll see forever.

In my eyes, in my words and in everything I do,

Nothing else but you

Ever!

(Tony)

And there's nothing for me but Maria,

Every sight that I see is Maria.

(Maria)

Tony, Tony...

....

Sí, ya vengo   *(Spanish)* Yes, I'm coming

(Tony)

 Always you, every thought I'll ever know,
 Everywhere I go, you'll be.

(Maria)

 All the world is only you and me! *(And now the buildings, the*
 world, fade away, leaving them suspended in space)
 Tonight, tonight,
 It all began tonight,
 I saw you and the world went away.
 Tonight, tonight,
 There's only you tonight,
 What are you, what you do, what you say.

(Tony)

 Today, all day I had the feeling
 A miracle would happen—
 I know now I was right.
 For here you are
 And what was just a world is a star
 Tonight!

(Both)

 Tonight, tonight,
 The world is full of light,
 With suns and moons all over the place.
 Tonight, tonight,
 The world is wild and bright,
 Going mad, shooting sparks into space.
 Today the world was just an address,
 A place for me to live in,
 No better than all right,
 But here you are
 And what was just a world is a star
 Tonight!

Scene from the film *West Side Story*

Man's Voice.

(*Offstage*) Maruca!

Maria.

Wait for me! (*She goes inside as the buildings begin to come back into place.*)

(**Tony** *sings*)

Tonight, tonight,

It all began tonight,

I saw you and the world went away.

Maria.

(*Returning*) I cannot stay. Go quickly!

Tony.

I'm not afraid.

Maria.

They are strict with me. Please.

Tony.

(*Kissing her*) Good night.

Maria.

Buenas noches.

Tony.

I love you.

Maria.

Yes, yes. Hurry. (*He climbs down.*) Wait! When will I see you?

(*He starts back up.*) No!

Tony.

Tomorrow.

Maria.

I work at the bridal shop. Come there.

....

buenas noches   (*Spanish*) good night

Tony.

At sundown.

Maria.

Yes. Good night.

Tony.

Good night. *(He starts off.)*

Maria.

Tony!

Tony.

Ssh!

Maria.

Come to the back door.

Tony.

Sí. (Again, he starts out.)

Maria.

Tony! *(He stops. A pause)* What does Tony stand for?

Tony.

Anton.

Maria.

Te adoro, Anton.

Tony.

Te adoro, Maria.

(Both *sing as music starts again)*

Good night, good night,

Sleep well and when you dream,

Dream of me

Tonight.

(She goes inside. He ducks out into the shadows.)

----

te adoro   *(Spanish)* I love you

Leonard Bernstein composed the music for *West Side Story.* Bernstein was a well-known U.S. conductor, composer, and pianist who was the Musical Director of the New York Philharmonic Orchestra from 1958–1969. He composed many types of music—for musical theater, opera, and films—and explained music in a clear and interesting manner for people who didn't know much about it.

Leonard Bernstein

Arthur Laurents began his career by writing radio plays.

Steven Sondheim

However, by 1945, he was well-known for his work on the script for *West Side Story,* which is based on Shakespeare's Romeo and Juliet.

Steven Sondheim, born in New York City, began his career as a lyric writer for *West Side Story.* He has had many successes since then, writing both lyrics and music for musical theater. He is known for his witty lyrics, complex melodies, and sophisticated plots. He won a Pulitzer Prize in 1985 for *Sunday in the Park with George.*

➤ **Leonard Bernstein (1918–1993)** ◄
➤ **Arthur Laurents (born 1918)** ◄
➤ **Steven Sondheim (born 1930)** ◄

➤ *What Do You Think?*

Think about the *West Side Story* scene and discuss it with your classmates and your teacher. Below are some questions to get you started. Try to use the text of the scene to support your ideas about it.

1. Retell the scene in your own words.
2. Why do you think these two young people fell in love?
3. Do you think their marriage could have succeeded?
4. Why does Maria say, "It is dangerous"? What do you think "it" refers to?
5. What is the mood of the first part of the scene? What emotions are expressed by the lyrics of the song, "Tonight?" Can you find specific quotes that reflect a change in tone from the first part of the scene to the last?
6. What effect does the balcony setting have on the scene? The New York City setting?

➤ *Background*

The balcony scene from *Romeo and Juliet* is probably the world's best known and most popular love scene. The play can be summarized as follows:

Romeo sees Juliet at a large formal dance at her father's house, and the two fall in love instantly. After they meet, each discovers the other is a member of an opposing family. In fact, the two families, the Montagues and the Capulets, have been feuding, or fighting, for many years. This discovery does not stop Romeo from secretly visiting Juliet. After the dance, he leaves his friends and goes to the Capulet's garden. There, under Juliet's balcony, Romeo overhears Juliet confess to the stars that she loves him. For the moment, love seems to conquer, but eventually the hatred between the two families destroys the young lovers.

Balcony Scene from Romeo and Juliet

by
William Shakespeare

Act II, scene 2
ROMEO, JULIET

(Capulet's orchard. Romeo advances from the wall.)

Romeo.
He jests at scars that never felt a wound.
(Juliet appears above at her window.)
But soft! What light through yonder window breaks?
It is the east, and Juliet is the sun!
Arise, fair sun, and kill the envious moon,
Who is already sick and pale with grief
That thou, her maid, art far more fair than she.
Be not her maid, since she is envious;
Her vestal livery is but sick and green,
And none but fools do wear it; cast it off.

....

jests   makes jokes
yonder   distant
envious   jealous
vestal   pure, virgin

Balcony Scene from *Romeo and Juliet,* Stratford Theater, 1974

It is my lady, O, it is my love!
Oh, that she knew she were!
She speaks, yet she says nothing; what of that?
Her eye discourses, I will answer it.—
I am too bold, 'tis not to me she speaks.
Two of the fairest stars in all the heaven,
Having some business, do entreat her eyes
To twinkle in their sphere till they return.
What if her eyes were there, they in her head?
The brightness of her cheek would shame those stars,
As daylight doth a lamp; her eyes in heaven
Would through the airy region stream so bright
That birds would sing and think it were not night.
See, how she leans her cheek upon her hand!
O, that I were a glove upon that hand,
That I might touch that cheek!

Juliet.

                    Ay me!

Romeo.

She speaks!
O, speak again, bright angel! For thou art
As glorious to this night, being o'er my head,
As a winged messenger of heaven
Unto the white-upturned wond'ring eyes
Of mortals that fall back to gaze on him

----

discourses   speaks, converses

entreat   beg

sphere   shape like a globe

doth   does

o'er   over

wond'ring   wondering, questioning

mortals   human beings

When he bestrides the lazy-pacing clouds
And sails upon the bosom of the air.

Juliet.

O Romeo, Romeo, wherefore art thou Romeo?
Deny thy father and refuse thy name.
Or, if thou wilt not, be but sworn my love
And I'll no longer be a Capulet.

Romeo.

(Aside) Shall I hear more, or shall I speak at this?

Juliet.

'Tis but thy name that is my enemy.
Thou art thyself, though not a Montague.
What's a Montague? It is nor hand, nor foot,
Nor arm, nor face, nor any other part
Belonging to a man, Oh, be some other name!
What's in a name? That which we call a rose
By any other name would smell as sweet;
So Romeo would, were he not Romeo call'd,
Retain that dear perfection which he owes
Without that title, Romeo, doff thy name,
And for thy name, which is no part of thee,
Take all myself.

Romeo.

I take thee at thy word.
Call me but love, and I'll be new baptiz'd;
Henceforth I never will be Romeo.

---

bestrides   sits upon, as on a horse
wherefore art thou   where are you
doff   take off, as a hat

Juliet.

What man art thou that, thus bescreen'd in night,
So stumblest on my counsel?

Romeo.

By a name
I know not how to tell thee who I am.
My name, dear saint, is hateful to myself,
Because it is an enemy to thee.
Had I written it, I would tear the word.

Juliet.

My ears have yet not drunk a hundred words
Of thy tongue's uttering, yet I know the sound.
Art thou not Romeo, and a Montague?

Romeo.

Neither, fair saint, if either thee dislike.

Juliet.

How cam'st thou hither, tell me, and wherefore?
The orchard walls are high and hard to climb,
And the place death, considering who thou art,
If any of my kinsmen find thee here.

Romeo.

With love's light wings did I o'erperch these walls;
For stony limits cannot hold love out.
And what love can do, that dares love attempt;
Therefore thy kinsmen are no stop to me.

---

bescreen'd hidden

counsel words, speech

uttering speaking

how cam'st thou hither? how did you come here?

kinsmen relatives

o'erperch climb over

Juliet.
If they do see thee, they will murder thee.
Romeo.
Alack, there lies more peril in thine eye
Than twenty of their swords. Look thou but sweet,
And I am proof against their enmity.
Juliet.
I would not for the world they saw thee here.
Romeo.
I have night's cloak to hide me from their eyes,
And but thou love me, let them find me here.
My life were better ended by their hate,
Than death prorogued, wanting of thy love.

....

peril   danger
enmity   hatred
prorogued   ended

★The remaining text for Act II, scene 2 of *Romeo and Juliet* can
be found in Appendix A (p. 234).

William Shakespeare, many say, was the most skilled *playwright,* or author of plays, the world has ever known. He wrote his plays, acted in them, and eventually became quite wealthy managing the theatre, too. His plays, written in poetic form, were often based on stories, myths, and legends that were well known in his time.

➤ **William Shakespeare (1564–1616)** ◄

AFTER YOU READ

➤ *What Do You Think?*

Think about the selection from *Romeo and Juliet* that you just read. Discuss it with your classmates and your teacher. Below are some questions to get you started. Try to use the text of the scene to support your ideas.

1. How does Romeo describe Juliet in his famous opening *soliloquy*—the speech he makes to himself when he is alone on the stage? To what objects does he compare her? From what perspectives does he see her?

2. Retell the scene in your own words. Ask for help from your teacher or a fellow classmate if you don't understand some of the language.

3. Juliet says, "Tis but thy name that is my enemy." Why do you think Romeo's name is her enemy? What is the importance of names? How would you react in this situation?

4. *West Side Story* and *Romeo and Juliet* are both set on balconies. What is the power of this setting? Why do you think the authors chose it?

5. The two scenes are set five hundred years and thousands of miles apart. How do you think the differences in setting influence the scenes?

6. Both *Romeo and Juliet,* a play, and *West Side Story,* a musical play, are told at least partly in poetry. Why do the writers of these love stories—and so many authors who write about love—use poetic forms?

➤ *Try This*

Comparing and Contrasting Literature Using a Venn Diagram **AM**

You used a Venn diagram in Unit 2 (p. 86) to compare two stories. A Venn diagram can also be used to compare certain elements—such as setting or character—in two pieces of literature. In the example on the next page, the settings from the two scenes you have just read are compared.

1. Work with a small group. In one circle, write "Balcony Scene from *West Side Story.*" In the second circle, write "Balcony Scene from *Romeo and Juliet.*" In the part of the circles that overlap, write "Both Scenes."

2. Choose an element of the two plays to compare and contrast. For example, choose plot, conflict, leads, conclusions, or metaphors.

3. Fill in the larger circles with information from and about each scene.

4. Look for ways the two are alike and fill in the middle section.

5. Prepare and present a discussion of your compare-and-contrast activity for the whole class. Use your Venn diagram as an illustration.

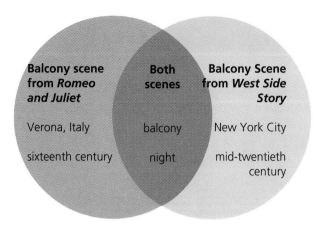

Balcony scene from *Romeo and Juliet*	Both scenes	Balcony Scene from *West Side Story*
Verona, Italy	balcony	New York City
sixteenth century	night	mid-twentieth century

➤ *Learning About Literature*

Alliteration

Alliteration is the repetition of the first, or initial, consonant sound in words that appear close together in a work of literature, usually in a poem. An example from *West Side Story* is "shooting sparks into space" (p. 151). With a partner, try to find two examples of alliteration in the scene from *Romeo and Juliet*.

Character Development **AM**

Writers develop characters in a variety of ways—by what the characters say, what the characters do, and what others say about the characters. In these two scenes, characters are revealed primarily by what they say and what their loved ones say about them.

Make a Venn diagram comparing and contrasting two characters, for example, Juliet and Maria, or Romeo and Tony. Prepare by reading both scenes carefully to find descriptions or actions of the characters. Then, put their char-

acteristics on the Venn diagram. Be sure to write in parentheses the page and line numbers of the scene where you found evidence of this characteristic.

➤ *Writing*

Comparing and Contrasting Two Characters **AM**

Use the information on one of the Venn diagrams to write a short essay comparing and contrasting the settings or two of the characters from the two balcony scenes. Use quotations from the scenes to support your ideas. Always put the speaker's words in quotation marks and be sure to tell who the speaker is. Use a slash (/) to show where a new line starts in a poem.

Below is an example of how to use a quotation from a play or a poem:

> Romeo thinks that Juliet is very beautiful. He compares her to the sun, and compares the brightness of her beauty to that of the sun compared to the moon. "Arise, fair sun, and kill the envious moon, / Who is already sick and pale with grief."

Unit Follow–Up

➤ Making Connections

Unit Project Ideas

Here are some possible unit projects. You may choose to think up a project of your own and check it out with your teacher. Use some of the strategies you learned in the unit to help you plan and complete your project. These include quickwrites, ranking ladders, charts, Think-Pair-Share, marking poems, Venn diagrams, brainstorming, imagery, and writing metaphors.

1. Love Songs. Copy down the words of several of your favorite love songs. Analyze the lyrics, or the words of the songs. You might include the following:

- interpretation of the lyrics in your own words
- discussion of symbols the songwriter uses
- discussion of the poet's use of rhyme, rhythm, or alliteration
- explanation of why you chose this song
- comparison of the song with a selection from the unit

2. Family Love Story. Most families have a funny or interesting love story that family members enjoy telling and hearing. The story may be about how family members met, what happened on their first date, how they decided to marry, or what their wedding was like. Write down, or transcribe, a love story from your family.

3. Lives of Writers. Read a biography of an author in the unit. Write about what things in a person's childhood might help make him or her grow up to be a writer.

4. Class Anthology of Love Poetry. Have each person in the class revise and edit a love poem or song he or she wrote during the unit. Publish the collection as a class anthology of love poetry. Include in your book a title page, copyright, dedication, introduction, and illustrations.

5. Art and Literature. Study your favorite work of fine art from the unit. Read about the artist. Write about what you see in the art work and why you like it. Relate the work to the literature it illustrates. Do they work well together? Why or why not?

6. Letter. Write a letter of appreciation to someone who has loved and supported you. Tell the story of how that person helped you and what it meant to you. If they are available, you might like to use a computer with word-processing software to help you revise and edit your letter. Some word processors come with software to check your grammar and spelling and even provide a thesaurus to help you with word choices.

Further Reading

Below are some materials related to this unit that you may enjoy.

• ***Art and Love: An Illustrated Anthology of Love Poetry,*** selected by Kate Farrell. The Metropolitan Museum of Art, 1990. Love poetry is grouped into themes such as, "The Mess of Love," "Go, Lovely Rose," and "The Marriage of True Minds." The poetry is illustrated with fine art from the permanent collection of the Metropolitan Museum.

• ***The Civil War,*** directed by Ken Burns. (Video) Beverly Hills, CA: Pacific Arts Video Publishing Co., 1990. This documentary series covers the Civil War with historical materials featuring the people, places, and events. Volume 1 includes a moving reading of the Sullivan Ballou letter.

• ***The Civil War: An American Tragedy,*** Franklin Watts Inc., 1992. This brief, attractive history depicts the Civil War with colorful maps, clear summary tables, and paintings and prints from the era.

• ***Favorite Tales from Shakespeare,*** by Bernard Miles. Rand McNally, 1976. Five of Shakespeare's plays, including *Romeo and Juliet,* are retold as lively short stories, richly illustrated by Victor G. Ambrus.

• ***The Land I Lost: Adventures of a Boy in Vietnam,*** by Huynh Quang Nhuong. Harper and Row, 1986. The author shares amazing and exciting childhood adventures of village life in Vietnam before the Vietnam War.

• ***Rise Up Singing,*** edited by Peter Blood-Patterson. Sing-Out, 1988. This sourcebook contains words, chords, and sources for over 1,200 songs, including about fifty love songs.

• ***Songs from This Earth on Turtle's Back,*** edited by Joseph Bruchac. Greenfield Review Press, 1983. Bruchac has collected representative selections from the work of important Native-American poets and has included photos of and biographical information about the poets.

• ***West Side Story,*** directed by Robert Wise and Jerome Robbins. (Video) Culver City, CA: MGM/UA Home video, 1988, copyright 1961. The dancing is thrilling in this video version of the Broadway musical. The story, based on Shakespeare's Romeo and Juliet, is about two young lovers from rival New York street gangs whose romance ends in tragedy.

Morning by Romare Bearden, 1979

4

Advice

In the stories, poems, and folktales that follow, the authors—or more often their characters—offer advice. They give the reader the opportunity to explore some of the questions literature has posed throughout the ages— what is important, what is honest, what is true, and what is a good life.

169

➤ *Exploring Your Own Experience*

Remembering—Four Share (AM)

Some people tie a string around a finger to help them remember important things; others make lists. What do you do?

1. Draw a picture or write about what you do to remember important things.
2. Now think of something in your life that you want to remember for a long time— perhaps something you will want to share with others in the future.
3. In groups of four, share your ideas about something you want to remember for a long time and your way of remembering it.

➤ *Background*

Because our world is always changing and renewing itself, our lives are often very different from those of our parents and grandparents. Sometimes we forget who we are, where we come from, and who has gone before us. Joy Harjo, a Creek Indian from Oklahoma, advises us to remember.

Remember

**by
Joy Harjo**

Remember the sky that you were born under,
know each of the star's stories.
Remember the moon, know who she is. I met her
in a bar once in Iowa City.
Remember the sun's birth at dawn, that is
the strongest point of time. Remember sundown
and the giving away to night.
Remember your birth, how your mother struggled
to give you form and breath. You are evidence of
her life, and her mother's, and hers.
Remember your father. He is your life, also.
Remember the earth whose skin you are:
red earth, black earth, yellow earth, white earth,
brown earth, we are earth.
Remember the plants, trees, animal life who all have their
tribes, their families, their histories, too. Talk to them,
listen to them. They are alive poems.

---

struggled fought, worked hard for
evidence proof

Woman and Blueberries by Patrick DesJarlait, 1972

Remember the wind. Remember her voice. She knows the origin of this universe. I heard her singing Kiowa war dance songs at the corner of Fourth and Central once.
Remember that you are all people and that all people are you.
Remember that you are this universe and that this universe is you.
Remember that all is in motion, is growing, is you.
Remember that language comes from this.
Remember the dance that language is, that life is.
Remember.

Kiowa   Native-American tribe from the southwestern U.S. They once hunted buffalo and were fierce warriors.

ABOUT THE AUTHOR

Joy Harjo was born in Tulsa, Oklahoma, and now lives in Santa Fe, New Mexico. She has written both collections of poetry

and screenplays that reflect her pride in being a Native-American from the Creek tribe, a woman, and an Oklahoman.

➤ **Joy Harjo (born 1951)** ◄

AFTER YOU READ

➤ *What Do You Think?*

Think about the poem and discuss it with your classmates and your teacher. Below are some questions to get you started. In your discussion, try to use the text of the poem to support your ideas.

1. To whom do you think the poet is speaking?
2. What does the speaker want the reader to remember? Make a list using your own words. Can you think of anything that all of these things have in common? Do they fall into any broad groups or categories?
3. Find a line from the poem that puzzles you. Read it aloud to the group and ask what the line means to them.
4. In the poem, there are many pairs of opposites, such as *mother/father* or *sun/moon*. What does the author want to accomplish by comparing these things?
5. How are language and life like a dance?

➤ *Try This*

Ranking Ladder AM

Make a ranking ladder using the things the poet asks the reader to remember in "Remember." A sample ranking ladder appears on the right.

1. Work with a partner.
2. Write each of the things the poet wants the reader to remember on a separate slip of paper.

3. Check your items with the poem. Have you included everything the poet mentions? Add any items you left out.
4. Group your items into larger categories. For example, *stars, moon,* and *sun* would be in the "heavenly bodies" category. Use slips of paper to label your categories.
5. Now take all of the larger categories and rank them on a ranking ladder, like the one below. Put the things that are most important to you at the top, the things that are least important at the bottom, and the others in between. Try to come to agreement with your partner.
6. Share your ranking ladder with another pair. Compare and contrast your ladders.

Ranking Ladder

Most Important

Least Important

➤ Learning About Literature

Repetition AM

In Unit 1 (p. 9), you studied repetition as a useful literary tool. In poetry, repetition can imitate the sound of something the poet is describing or add a musical quality to the poem. Try answering the following questions to better understand the use of repetition in the poem "Remember."

1. What words are repeated in the poem?
2. What sentence patterns are repeated?
3. What words are repeated in combination with different words?
4. What is the effect of this repetition?
5. Does the repetition create a musical quality?

➤ Writing

Repetition AM

Write a poem that offers advice. Use one of the following words or phrases to begin each line of your poem, or choose a word or phrase of your own.

Remember:

Forget:

Do:

Do not:

Seek:

Watch out for:

➤ Exploring Your Own Experience

Rules AM

The last poem instructed the reader to do something—to remember certain things. Other advice, advice that we sometimes prefer not to listen to, can be given in rules that tell us what we shouldn't do. What are some of these rules, or "don'ts," that you often hear at home or at school? Brainstorm for a while and create a class list of these "don'ts." Have one classmate write the class ideas on the board.

➤ Background

Poets often surprise readers by giving them something they don't expect. See if Karla Kuskin's "rules" are what you expect.

Rules

by
Karla Kuskin

Do not jump on ancient uncles.
Do not yell at average mice.
Do not wear a broom to breakfast.
Do not ask a snake's advice.
Do not bathe in chocolate pudding.
Do not talk to bearded bears.
Do not smoke cigars on sofas.

ancient   very old

Three Musicians by Pablo Picasso, 1921

Do not dance on velvet chairs.
Do not take a whale to visit
Russell's mother's cousin's yacht.
And whatever else you do do
It is better you
Do not.

....

yacht   large, fancy sailing boat

ABOUT THE AUTHOR

Karla Kuskin created her first poem when she was four years old—she dictated it to her mother before she knew how to write. Since then, she has written and illustrated more than twenty-five books for children, and has written many more with the help of other illustrators. She has also written screenplays and articles about writing and teaching poetry. Kuskin often visits schools to help young people with writing.

➤ **Karla Kuskin (born 1932)** ◄

➤ *What Do You Think*

Think about the poem and discuss it with your classmates and your teacher. Below are some questions to get you started. In your discussion, try to use the text of the poem to support your ideas.

1. Are there similarities between the rules in Kuskin's poem and the rules you wrote down before reading it?
2. Are Kuskin's rules surprising in any way?
3. Do the rules from Kuskin's poem seem funny to you? Why or why not?
4. Which of Kuskin's rules is your favorite?
5. Which of the rules offers what you think is good advice? Why do you think so?

➤ *Try This*

Ironic or Metaphorical Advice **AM**

Karla Kuskin's rules can be read as *ironic*—as making fun of rules. They can also be read as *metaphorical*. If the rules are seen as metaphors, they may hold some good advice for us. For example, "Do not jump on ancient uncles" might mean "Pay attention to the wisdom of the past." "Do not wear a broom to breakfast" might mean "There is a time for work and a time to be with your family. Do not try to combine them." Look for metaphorical meanings in other lines of the poem, "Rules."

Now, try to write your own metaphorical or ironic rules.

1. Work in small groups.
2. Review the list of rules you made before reading the poem.
3. Review the types of irony used in literature (p. 17).
4. Review the meaning of metaphor (p. 134).
5. Each group takes two or three of the rules and rewrites them into an ironic or metaphorical rule like one of Kuskin's. Some of these hints for rewriting might help:
   - Write the opposite.
   - Put the rule in an unusual setting.
   - Make the rule about an animal.
6. Read your new rules out loud to your group. Discuss revisions to make them sound better or funnier or to make the words more interesting. Use a thesaurus if needed.
7. Rewrite your revised rules. Edit, illustrate, and publish them as a class display or book.

Rhyme Scheme

Kuskin's use of rhyme, rhythm, and repetition makes her poem memorable. Use letters to write the rhyme scheme of the poem "Rules." Refer to page 107 if you need to review rhyme scheme.

Poetic Feet **AM**

You have already learned that lines of poetry have rhythm—patterns of stressed and unstressed syllables. A *foot* is a basic unit of meter that gives a poem, or part of a poem, a particular rhythm. There are several types of feet; however, three of the most common are *iambic foot, trochaic foot,* and *dactylic foot.* The pattern of accented and unaccented syllables helps you to figure out the type of foot the poet uses. Remember that accent marks are used to label a syllable as stressed (/) or unstressed (˘). Review rhyme scheme on page 107, if you need to. Then look at the examples below of the three types of meter:

Iambic foot (˘/):

"Wĕ weár thĕ másk thăt gríns ănd líes, Ĭt hídes oŭr cheéks ănd shádes oŭr eyés—" (from "We Wear the Mask").

Trochaic foot (/˘):

"Ońce ŭpón ă mídnĭght dréarў, whĭle Ĭ pónderĕd, wéak ănd weárў," (from "The Raven").

Dactylic foot (/˘˘):

"Spínăch, ŏh Spínăch, Ĭ háte yŏu, yoŭ're gróss. Yoú aře thĕ kínd ŏf fŏod Í hăte thĕ móst."

1. Work in small groups.
2. Copy "Rules" onto a piece of paper. Each person should have a copy of the poem.
3. Listen as someone reads the poem, one line at a time, as others mark accented and unaccented syllables.
4. Try to decide which type of poetic feet each poem has.

➤ *Writing*

Humorous Advice **AM**

1. As a class, collect and read aloud advice columns from the newspaper. What kinds of problems do people write about?
2. Each person in the class writes an "advice column" question on a slip of paper. Put them in a hat.
3. Each person draws a question from the hat, and writes a humorous response to the question.
4. Share your first draft with a group of peers.
5. Revise your responses. Then post them on a classroom wall, read them aloud in class, or publish them in a class newspaper.

➤ Exploring Your Own Experience AM

Interviews—What Is A True Friend?

1. Interview five people. Ask them, "What is a true friend?" Take notes on their answers.
2. Report your answers to the class.
3. Make a class summary of your findings. Use a Cluster Map (p. 88), a Character Web (p. 80), or a Sunshine Outline (p. 32).

➤ Background

Rulers, princes, and rich men in ancient Egypt were called "sultans." The next story tells of how a future sultan's mother helped her son to learn how to choose his friends.

This *folktale* is from Egypt. Folktales are traditionally passed from person to person and from generation to generation through story telling, as part of a culture's oral tradition. Often folktales have a message, or advice, for listeners or readers. Perhaps those who tell the following folktale want their listeners to learn something about what a true friend should be.

A Mother's Advice

Retold by
Ahmed and Zane Zagbul

Once there was a sultan who died and left his young son Selim to rule over his kingdom. Luckily, Selim's mother was very smart and gave her son good advice. She told him that he would grow up to be a sultan like his father but that there were many things he had to learn first.

"Some people will want to be around you because of your money, and some will want to be around you because of your power. Not too many people will seek you just because of your person," she taught him. The boy asked his mother how he would know the difference between someone who was a true friend and someone who had ulterior motives.

His mother suggested a simple plan: Whenever you make a friend, she said, ask the new friend to come over to breakfast. At breakfast offer three hard-boiled eggs. If the friend eats one and leaves two, then he is false because he just wants to seem like he cares more about you than himself. If he eats two and leaves one, forget him too because he is greedy and has no manners. A true friend will share equally with you.

---

sultan   an Islamic ruler or prince
ulterior   hidden
motives   reasons for doing things

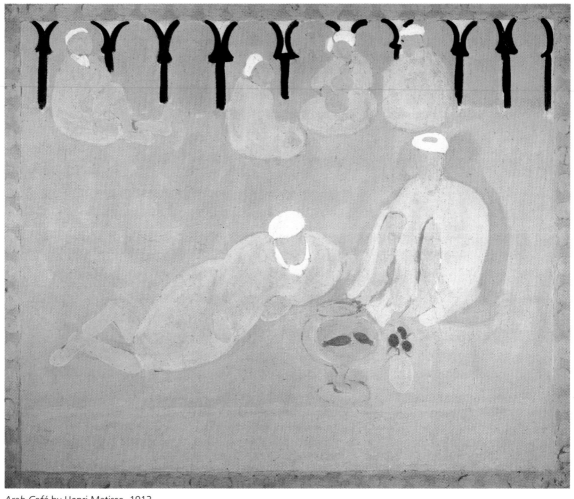

Arab Café by Henri Matisse, 1913

The first friend Selim invited to breakfast was the son of an important government official. Three eggs were served, and after each boy had had one, the visitor insisted that Selim eat the third egg. Selim recognized his false generosity and told

----

generosity   kindness, giving nature

the boy goodbye. The second visitor was the mayor's son. Again three eggs were served; after each boy had eaten one, the visitor ate the third egg without even asking Selim if he wanted it. It was clear that he was not the right friend either.

Selim was still hoping to find a good friend. One day he decided to go among the poor people to try to find a companion, and he met a woodcutter's son who was dressed in rags. He wore clumsy boots and had rough hands from working hard. Selim invited him to come over, and the boy invited him to his house as well. This friend lived in a small hut, and when Selim went there, they shared meager meals of bread and salt or bread and oil; sometimes they grilled corn on the cob, and it was delicious.

When the boy finally came over to breakfast at Selim's palace, Selim was very nervous to see what he would do when the three eggs were served. Selim held his breath as the woodcutter's son got out his knife and cut the third egg in two. "You eat one egg and a half, and I will eat one egg and a half," the friend said.

Selim was overjoyed, for he had found his true friend. When he told his mother about it, she said, "This is the friend who likes you for yourself. Cherish and honor this friendship."

And Selim did as his mother said. Selim and the woodcutter's son became best friends. When he grew up and became sultan, Selim made his friend his number-one assistant, and they enjoyed a life-long, sincere, and loving friendship.

....

clumsy	without grace, awkward
meager	small, scant
cherish	care for tenderly, treat carefully
sincere	true, honest

AFTER YOU READ

▶ *What Do You Think?*

Think about the story and discuss it with your classmates and your teacher. Below are some questions to get you started. In your discussion, try to use the text of the story to support your ideas.

1. What was the test for true friendship that Selim's mother suggested? Did the test work for Selim?
2. What was Selim's goal? How many times did he try to reach that goal?
3. Is there any unexpected element or surprise in the story? If so, discuss it.

4. What do you think this story is trying to teach? Could you state a moral, or lesson, to this story in one sentence?
5. How does the storyteller describe the characters in the story? Does the storyteller use many details? Are the characters complex?

▶ *Try This*

Story Map AM

Use a story map like the one below to outline the main elements of "A Mother's Advice."

Story Map of "A Mother's Advice"	
Story Elements:	**Elements in "A Mother's Advice"**
Characters:	
Setting:	
Initial Event:	
Reaction:	
Goal-setting:	
Attempt to Reach Goal:	
Outcome:	
Resolution:	

➤ *Learning About Literature*

The Number Three in Folktales

The number three often appears in literature, especially in folktales. You may be familiar with the story of "The Three Bears," whose breakfasts were "too hot," "too cold," or "just right." You may have heard a version of "Cinderella," in which there were three daughters. Two of the daughters were ugly in both appearance and action. The third daughter was both beautiful and kind.

Often in the teaching of folktales, there is a search for a balance between extremes. In "A Mother's Advice," Selim seeks a friend who is neither insincerely generous, nor greedy, but instead one who is balanced between the two extremes.

Think of a folktale that you know in which something comes in threes. If you can't think of one, ask your teacher, your friends, your librarian, or family members for suggestions. Talk about these folktales in class. Make a chart of folktales that have the 'three' pattern. Discuss how the third element in these stories is different and important.

Static and Dynamic Characters AM

Folktales often include *static characters* or characters who do not change in the story. Other characters' personalities or ideas change during the action of a folktale, a story, a poem, or a novel. These characters are called *dynamic characters*. Change in the characters adds to the interest and complexity of a story.

1. Are the characters static or dynamic in "A Mother's Advice?" Give evidence from the story.
2. Look back over other stories in this book, and others you have read. Find static characters and dynamic characters. Which characters do you think are the most interesting? Why? The chart on the next page can help you decide if characters you have read about are static or dynamic.

Static and Dynamic Characters

Character:	Character's personality and actions at beginning of the story:	Character's personality and actions at end of the story:	Dynamic or Static:
Lorena, in "The Raiders Jacket"	Lorena gets excited when Eddie loans her his jacket.	Lorena turns away from romance and buys a practical gift for her mother.	Dynamic
Rachel, in "Eleven"			
The wise woman, in "The Wise Woman of Córdoba"			
Selim, in "A Mother's Advice"			

➤ *Writing*

Writing about Characterization (AM)

1. Select a favorite character from a story in this book.
2. Fill out a section in the Static and Dynamic Characters Chart for this character. Decide if your favorite character is static or dynamic.
3. Write a short essay about this character. Start your essay with a *thesis statement,* or a statement of your main idea. The thesis should state whether you think the character is static or dynamic. Then support your thesis in the body of the essay by giving details that describe the character at the beginning and at the end of the story. Finally, at the end of your essay, restate your thesis in a different way. Look back at Unit 1 (p. 53) if you need more information on writing an essay.
4. Use the steps of the writing process to revise and polish your essay.

➤ Exploring Your Own Experience

Ways of Speaking English

As you have probably noticed, people speak English in many different ways. Groups of people use different accents—ways of pronouncing sounds. People also use different *dialects,* forms of speech used in a region of a country or by a group of people. Have you also noticed that people use English differently in different situations? For example, when people play sports with their friends, they use English differently than they do in a job interview.

1. Today, pay special attention to the way people around you use English. Is their language formal or informal? How do they pronounce words? Do they use slang? Do they speak in sentences or in phrases? Do they use standard English grammar like that used in school and in textbooks?

2. Make a list of the different places or situations where people use a specific kind of English. Then try to give a name to that kind of language.

3. List the ways of speaking English in the first column of a chart like the one below.

4. In the second column, tell where that way of using English works best.

5. In the third column, tell where that way of using English would not work well.

Several examples are found below.

➤ Background

In the following poem, Langston Hughes writes with the voice of a hard-working African-American mother offering advice to her son.

Ways of Speaking English

Way of speaking:	Where it works best:	Where it wouldn't work well:
baby talk	with babies	in the principal's office
casual language (dropping g from ing, using phrases, not sentences)	with friends at home	in a term paper or in a speech
very formal and polite language	at a job interview	in a basketball game

Mother to Son

by
Langston Hughes

Well, son, I'll tell you;
Life for me ain't been no crystal stair.
It's had tacks in it,
And splinters,
And boards torn up,
And places with no carpet on the floor—
Bare.
But all the time
I'se been a–climbin' on,
And reachin' landin's,
And turnin' corners,
And sometimes goin' in the dark
Where there ain't been no light.
So boy, don't you turn back.

---

crystal   very clear, bright glass
splinters   small, thin, sharp pieces of wood
I'se been a-climbin'   I've been climbing

Woman in Calico by William H. Johnson, 1944

Don't you set down on the steps
'Cause you finds it's kinder hard.
Don't you fall now—
For I'se still goin', honey,
I'se still climbin',
And life for me ain't been no crystal stair.

....

kinder   kind of
I'se   I'm

➤ *What Do You Think?*

Think about the story and discuss it with your classmates and your teacher. Below are some questions to get you started. In your discussion, try to use text from the story to support your ideas.

1. What does the mother in the poem compare life to?
2. What are some of the details of this comparison?
3. How do you imagine 'the stairway of life'?
4. Can you think of any other way to say, "Life ain't been no crystal stair?"
5. What does the mother advise the son to do?
6. Do you agree with the mother that "life ain't no crystal stair?" Based on your own experience, to what would you compare life?

➤ *Try This*

Drawing Life's Stairway **AM**

1. Draw a stairway (or a road, a path, or walkway) that reflects your view of what life is like.
2. When you finish, write a short description of what you drew. The following questions might help you.
   - Are there twists and turns?
   - Are all the steps the same height?
   - Is the part of the stairway in the future different from the part of the stairway in the past?
3. Share your drawings and thoughts with your classmates.

➤ *Learning About Literature*

Analogy

You have already studied two types of literary comparisons, simile and metaphor. Sometimes poets use a longer, more extended comparison of two things, called an *analogy*. The entire poem "Mother to Son" compares life to a stairway. For an analogy to work, the two subjects being compared must have some characteristics in common. Both similes and metaphors can be used to express analogies in poetry.

Discuss the following questions about "Mother to Son."

1. What do the two things being compared, life and a stairway, have in common?
2. What metaphors are used to express the analogy?
3. In your opinion, is this an effective analogy? Why or why not?

Dialect

Dialect is a variety of a language spoken by a particular group. Most languages have different dialects. "Mother to Son" is written in an African-American dialect of English.

In Unit 3, you learned about poetic license, the freedom that poets have to change facts and vary the rules of English. In communication, such as speeches, research papers, and newspaper articles, standard English is almost always used. In poetry and some fiction, however, use of nonstandard dialects can be very effective.

Some of the signs that this poem uses nonstandard language are the dropped *"g's"* on *"ing"* words, and the use of the word *"ain't"*. Can you find other evidence of dialect in the poem? How do you think the use of dialect adds to the poem? Can you find other literary selections that use dialect? Why do you think the author chose to write his poem in a dialect?

➤ *Writing*

Using Analogies AM

Use an analogy to write about something that interests you. For example, you might compare the following:

- a solar system to an atom
- a complex traffic intersection to a plate of spaghetti
- a friendship to a road
- a fight to a storm
- an animal to a machine

Use the steps of the writing process to share, revise, and polish your writing.

➤ *Exploring Your Own Experience*

Proverbs **AM**

Every culture has sayings or *proverbs*—colorful phrases to pass on some teaching. The meaning of proverbs is usually not *literal,* but *figurative.* *Literal meaning* is the exact meaning of the words. *Figurative* meaning is meaning that uses metaphor, simile, or some other figure of speech. The meanings of proverbs differ from the usual (literal) meaning of the words. Proverbs usually include figurative language, such as metaphors or similes. In the chart below are some examples of proverbs or sayings and their meanings. Collect others that you hear in conversations and from resource books in the library. Each person can choose one of the proverbs to explain, and perhaps illustrate it with a picture. Feel free to include proverbs you know in other languages.

➤ *Background*

In pairs, try to guess what the following three proverbs mean. Check your answers with the rest of the class and your teacher.

- Handsome is as handsome does.
- Actions speak louder than words.
- Beauty is only skin deep.

Proverbs Chart

Proverb or saying	Illustration	Meaning
That's like taking candy from a baby.		That's very easy.
She speaks with a forked tongue.		She doesn't tell the truth.
A stitch in time saves nine.		If you do something right away, it takes less time in the end.

Conceit

by
Elizabeth Ruiz

Reflection by G.G. Kopilak, 1979

I looked in the mirror.
Handsome is as handsome does, I thought.
So I decided to do something handsome
Because actions speak louder than words.
After acting handsome,
I looked in the mirror again.
Beauty is only skin deep. I thought,
I must have thick skin.

conceit   pride, vanity, thinking highly of oneself

➤ *What Do You Think?*

Think about the poem and discuss it with your classmates and your teacher. Below are some questions to get you started. In your discussion, try to use the text of the poem to back up your ideas about it.

1. What do you think the speaker wanted to see in the mirror?
2. Why did the speaker decide to do something handsome?
3. What was the result of doing something handsome?
4. Why does the speaker conclude that he/she has thick skin?
5. Do you think the speaker is male or female? Why?
6. Why do you think the poem is titled "Conceit?"

➤ *Try This*

Proverb Practice

Write each proverb you have collected, including the ones in the poem "Conceit," on an index card. Use one color marker for the proverbs. Write the meaning of each proverb on a different index card. Use a different color marker for the meanings. Use the cards to play Concentration.

1. Play this game in a group of about four.
2. Spread all the cards on a table face down.
3. Each person takes a turn trying to turn over cards that match a proverb to a meaning. Use the proverbs chart to check answers.
4. If a person finds a match, he/she can have another turn. If the person fails to find a match, it is the next person's turn. Continue around the group.
5. When all the proverbs have been matched to their meanings, count cards. The person with the most is the winner.

➤ Learning About Literature

What is a Cliché?

Clichés are phrases that are so common and expected that they are not interesting to the reader. Examples are: "It was as green as grass," or "It was a dark and stormy night." Writing teachers often encourage writers *not* to use clichés. In the poem "Conceit," Elizabeth Ruiz uses proverbs that are so common that some people might call them clichés. However, she uses them in a new and surprising way by combining them and by including them in a "story" about someone looking in a mirror. Ruiz demonstrates that it is more important to use words in interesting ways than it is just to avoid clichés. If you want your writing to be interesting, always try to write in a way that is a little bit new and different.

➤ Writing

Using Proverbs AM

1. Combine two or more of the proverbs from *Exploring Your Own Experience* on your chart to create your own poem or short story. Try to combine them in a surprising way.

2. Use the steps of the writing process to share, revise, edit, and perhaps publish your work.

➤ *Exploring Your Own Experience*

Learning from Mistakes **AM**

When you were a young child, you probably made mistakes or did things that you didn't really understand were wrong. If you were lucky, you learned from the experience and didn't make the same mistake again.

1. Use your own experience and stories you have read to describe some of the mistakes children make because they don't know any better.

2. As you offer ideas, have someone in your class write them on a chart or on the board.

3. Use the chart to remind you of a story about you or other family members.

4. In groups of four, share your stories.

➤ *Background*

The 1930s was the time of The Great Depression in the U.S. Life was very difficult, and many people did not have jobs or money. The Works Projects Administration (WPA) was part of the New Deal laws passed by the U.S. Congress in 1935 to help give jobs to over 8.5 million people. Workers were hired to build highways, streets, bridges, and parks. The WPA also created work for artists, writers, actors, and musicians. The father in the next story has a WPA job as a "pick-y-pala," or a worker with a pick and shovel.

La Peseta (The Quarter)

**From *Stories from El Barrio*
by Piri Thomas**

I

A child wants to have a few *centavos*
Some *dinero* to be able to go to the movies
To be able to buy a hot dog or a *bacalaito*.
You know, things that other people
Who have wealth can enjoy.
To have some money in your pocket
That's a joy indeed.
You can go into the candy store
Instead of standing outside deciding
Whether to keep on walking
Or snatch a candy bar, very cool and undetected.

II

My father worked very hard on the WPA
Construction gang with *pick-y-pala*, shovel,
Digging very deep holes and filling them up too.
When he left for *trabajo* in the morning

---

centavos   *(Spanish)* cents
dinero   *(Spanish)* money
bacalaito   *(Spanish)* salt cod fish
undetected   not found out, undiscovered
trabajo   *(Spanish)* work

Construction of a Dam (Mural study, Department of the Interior)
by William Gropper, 1937

He would give my mother money to buy food,
Always leaving something extra on top of the table
To make sure that we'd also have dessert.
On this day, he put one quarter, some dimes, and a nickel,
Maybe forty-five or fifty cents, a whole lot.
I really wanted to go to that movie
With my new girlfriend named Cándida.
I looked at the money and said,
"Well, they would not miss it, you know."
So I took the quarter and put it into my socks,
Pushing it all the way down until it was underneath—inside my sneaker.

III

As my father started to walk out the door
To go to his job of *pick-y-pala*,
He said to my mother,
"I left some change."
And my mother said, "Bring it to me."
My father came back for the money,
And he looked and he quietly said, "There is a quarter missing."
Oh, if he had only gone, I thought,
Then Mama would not have known a quarter was missing.

IV

I immediately began to look all over the floor
And under the beds and over everything.
And my father just stood there,
Looking at me.
I, who always complained
About going down to the grocery store
Or even washing behind my ears,

I, who always was the last to volunteer,
Was all of a sudden so fantastically willing
To look for the missing *peseta*.

V

My father said to my sister,
"Have you seen the quarter?"
My sister said, "No."
My father said to me,
"Have you seen it?"
And I said, "No, Poppa,
Can't you see I'm trying hard to find it?"
I was really wishing I had never taken
That *maldita peseta*.
I was not born a criminal,
I just wanted a chance to see what it was like
To have a quarter.

VI

My father looked at me,
And I knew that he knew
That the quarter was somewhere on me.
But not to make me feel completely guilty,
He said, "I'll frisk everybody."
Leaving me there sweating to the last—till
Finally, it was my turn.
"Let me see your pants, son."
I took them off.
He emptied my pockets

---

volunteer   offer to do something

fantastically   amazingly, unbelievably

maldita   *(Spanish)* cursed, evil

frisk   search a person by feeling his or her clothing

And while he was doing all this frisking,
I was loudly proclaiming my innocence
complete with crossing *corazón*.
"Poppa, how could you even think this?"
"Poppa, have you ever known me to take anything
That didn't belong to me?"

VII

While in my mind justifying it,
As part of my inheritance.
Poppa said, "Take off your sneakers."
I took my smelly sneakers off.
Poppa beat them hard against each other—
    I was so glad it wasn't my *cabeza*.
He said, "Your socks."
So I took one sock off.
The sock with the quarter was the last to go.
I slipped it off, holding the coin inside
With my thumb and forefinger,
And praying to all the Gods in Heaven
That the quarter would stay in the sock,
Which it did not.
Plink-ling-ling the quarter came tumbling out.
My face said, "How in the hell did that get there?"
I tried to smile, but that didn't work.

---

proclaiming   announcing, stating loudly

innocence   state of being not guilty or free from wrongdoing

corazón   *(Spanish)* heart

justifying   defending, making it sound right

inheritance   money passed down by family

cabeza   *(Spanish)* head

Boy in Blue (Niño en azul) by Rufino Tamayo, 1928

VIII

My father dove straight for me
As I dove under the bed.
My father could not get under it because it was
a very low bed.
So he proceeded very calmly
To take the mattress off.
In the background, my mother seemed undecided
on child-abuse, 'cause she was saying,
"Don't hit him on the head.
Because you can make him *loco*.
If you got to hit him,
Around the legs is good enough.
Don't hit him in the head.
I want him to be *inteligente* when he grows up."
I cringed in terror—suppose Poppa broke my legs.

IX

My father ripped off the springs
And then removed his pants belt.
It looked bigger than the whip
That Zorro used to make his mark.
I broke into a run.
I became the greatest quarterback in the world.
My father went for me
And I ducked him, cut, and split,

---

dove   jumped head-first into something

proceeded   went forward, continued

loco   *(Spanish)* crazy

inteligente   *(Spanish)* smart, intelligent

cringed   hung back, hid

Zorro   Mexican T.V. and film character

cut   turned a sharp corner

Ran, stopped on a dime, and
Returned nine cents change.
I wondered if Poppa would believe that *peseta*
had just rolled off the table
And without me feeling a thing had slipped into
    my sock and wormed its way under my foot.

X

My father came after me like Superman,
Faster than a speeding bullet, more powerful
Than a locomotive, able to leap backyard fences
In a single bound.
He was a natural-born athlete
Who played for the Cuban Stars, the Black Stars,
The Puerto Rican stars—*Olé, olé.*
I had to beat my father running,
And then—I was caught.
I tried to smile as I waited for the blows that were to come,
But my father just looked at me and said,
"Son, why didn't you ask for it?

---

stopped on a dime *(idiom)* stopped very quickly
wormed crawled or crept, wiggled
Olé, olé *(Spanish)* "hurray!", a Spanish cheer

I would have given it to you.
Did you have to steal it?"
I just looked at Poppa and began to cry.
My sorry tears ran down my cheeks.
I just stood there feeling like a chump.
What can a guy say at a time like that?

---

chump   foolish person

ABOUT THE AUTHOR

Piri Thomas was born in New York City and grew up in Spanish Harlem, a region of New York City where many Puerto Ricans lived at the time. In his youth, Thomas got involved in gangs and drugs, and spent seven years in prison. After he got out,

he returned to his old neighborhood to work with young people, and later he helped create a program for former drug addicts in Puerto Rico called "New Breed." Thomas has written an *autobiography*, fiction, a play, and many articles.

➤ **Piri Thomas (born 1928)** ◄

➤ *What Do You Think?*

Think about the poem and discuss it with your classmates and your teacher. Below are some questions to get you started. In your discussion, try to use the text of the story to support your ideas.

1. Why did the boy feel he needed the quarter? Do you think he had a good reason to take it? Why or why not?

2. How did the boy first try to hide the fact that he had taken the quarter? Did he fool anyone? How do you know?

3. What does the story tell you about the family? What is their financial situation?

4. What sort of parent was the mother? The father? Find parts of the story to support your opinion.

5. The boy tells the story in a humorous way. One of the sources of humor is exaggeration, or making something larger or more important than it really is. Find and read aloud passages that you think are humorous. Does the author use exaggeration in these passages?

6. Is "La Peseta" a story or a poem? Why do you think so?

7. How do you feel about the ending of the story?

8. What advice do you think the author offers the reader in this story?

➤ *Try This*

Idioms

Piri Thomas uses many colorful *idioms*. An idiom is an interesting phrase or expression whose meaning cannot be understood from the ordinary meaning of the words in it. For example, one of the idioms from "La Peseta" is "stopped on a dime."

1. As you hear idioms in conversations or see them when you read, write the idioms and their meanings on self-stick notes.

2. Make a class chart of idioms in English and other languages by arranging the self-stick notes in alphabetical order on the classroom wall.

3. Refer to the chart when you need to check the meanings of idioms. Add new idioms to the chart when you find them.

➤ *Learning About Literature*

Narrative and Lyric Poems **AM**

"La Peseta" is a poem that is also a story. Poems that tell a story are called *narrative* poems. However, most of the poems you have read in this book are *lyric* poems—poems that express the poet's personal emotions or sentiments rather than tell of events. A love poem, a patriotic song, an ode, and a hymn are all types of lyric poems. Look back over all the poems you have read in this book. Which of those poems do you think are narrative? Which are lyric? Read lines of poems that support your decision.

➤ *Writing*

Lessons from Childhood **AM**

Write an account of an event in your childhood that taught you something. You might choose to write down the story you shared before reading "La Peseta" in *Exploring Your Own Experience* (p. 200). You may want to use a story map to outline the elements of your story. You can choose to tell your story in prose or in the form of a narrative poem. To make your language colorful, try to include some of the English idioms you have collected. Use the steps of the writing process to share, revise, and edit your work.

➤ *Exploring Your Own Experience*

Round Table

1. Work in a group of four to six.
2. Someone can volunteer to be the note-taker. Go around the circle clockwise with each person telling something he or she does well. The note-taker should write down all of the ideas.
3. You may want to go around the circle several times to create a very long list.
4. When you have finished, the note-taker should read the list aloud.
5. Discuss how it feels to be good at something. Discuss how you think you got that way.

➤ *Background*

The story that follows is about a girl who was very good at chess. It is taken from a novel by Amy Tan called *The Joy Luck Club,* which was made into a popular movie. Tan is the American-born daughter of Chinese parents. In her moving novel, Tan explores the different relationships of four pairs of Chinese-American daughters and their Chinese mothers.

Four Directions

**From *The Joy Luck Club*
by Amy Tan**

I was ten years old. Even though I was young, I knew my ability to play chess was a gift. It was effortless, so easy. I could see things on the chessboard that other people could not. I could create barriers to protect myself that were invisible to my opponents. And this gift gave me supreme confidence. I knew what my opponents would do, move for move. I knew at exactly what point their faces would fall when my seemingly simple and childlike strategy would reveal itself as a devastating and irrevocable course. I loved to win.

And my mother loved to show me off, like one of my many trophies she polished. She used to discuss my games as if she had devised the strategies.

"I told my daughter, use your horses to run over the enemy," she informed one shopkeeper. "She won very quickly this way." And of course, she had said this before the game—that and a hundred other useless things that had nothing to do with my winning.

To our family friends who visited she would confide: "You don't have to be so smart to win chess. It is just tricks. You blow from the North, South, East, and West. The other person becomes confused. They don't know which way to run."

---

barriers   blocks, walls
supreme   total, maximum, complete
confidence   faith in oneself
devastating   crushing, very harmful
irrevocable   final, irreversible

devised   created, made up
confide   tell secretly

From "The Joy Luck Club", Copyright © 1993 Buena Vista

I hated the way she tried to take all the credit. And one day I told her so, shouting at her on Stockton Street, in the middle of a crowd of people. I told her she didn't know anything, so she shouldn't show off. She should shut up. Words to that effect.

That evening and the next day she wouldn't speak to me. She would say stiff words to my father and brothers, as if I had become invisible and she was talking about a rotten fish she had thrown away but which had left behind its bad smell.

I knew this strategy, the sneaky way to get someone to pounce back in anger and fall into a trap. So I ignored her. I refused to speak and waited for her to come to me.

After many days had gone by in silence, I sat in my room, staring at the sixty-four squares of my chessboard, trying to think of another way. And that's when I decided to quit playing chess.

Of course I didn't mean to quit forever. At most, just for a few days. And I made a show of it. Instead of practicing in my room every night, as I always did, I marched into the living room and sat down in front of the television set with my brothers, who stared at me, an unwelcome intruder. I used my brothers to further my plan; I cracked my knuckles to annoy them.

"Ma!" they shouted. "Make her stop. Make her go away."

But my mother did not say anything.

Still I was not worried. But I could see I would have to make a stronger move. I decided to sacrifice a tournament that was coming up in one week. I would refuse to play in it. And my mother would certainly have to speak to me about this. Because the sponsors and the benevolent associations would start calling her, asking, shouting, pleading to make me play again.

And then the tournament came and went. And she did not come to me, crying, "Why are you not playing chess?" But I was crying inside, because I learned that a boy whom I

---

stiff rigid, formal
rotten old and spoiled, bad-smelling
strategy plan of attack
pounce jump on something quickly

intruder unwanted person, meddler
sacrifice give up
benevolent associations organizations that try to create good will toward a group of people
pleading begging

Ladies Playing Double Sixes. Style of Chou Fang. China, Song dynasty, 10th/11th Century

had easily defeated on two other occasions had won.

I realized my mother knew more tricks than I had thought. But now I was tired of her game. I wanted to start practicing for the next tournament. So I decided to pretend to let her win. I would be the one to speak first.

"I am ready to play chess again," I announced to her. I had imagined she would smile and then ask me what special thing I wanted to eat.

But instead, she gathered her face into a frown and stared into my eyes, as if she could force some kind of truth out of me.

"Why do you tell me this?" she finally said in sharp tones. "You think it is so easy. One day quit, next day play. Everything for you is this way. So smart, so easy, so fast."

"I said I'll play," I whined.

"No!" she shouted, and I almost jumped out of my scalp. "It is not so easy anymore."

I was quivering, stunned by what she said, in not knowing what she meant. And then I went back to my room. I stared at my chessboard, its sixty-four squares, to figure out how to undo this terrible mess. And after staring like this for many hours, I actually believed that I had made the white squares black and the black squares white, and everything would be all right.

And sure enough, I won her back. That night I developed a high fever, and she sat next to my bed, scolding me for going to school without my sweater. In the morning she was there as well, feeding me rice porridge flavored with chicken broth she had strained herself. She said she was feeding me this because I had the chicken pox and one chicken knew how to fight another. And in the afternoon, she sat in a chair in my room, knitting me a pink sweater while telling me about a sweater that Auntie Suyuan had knit for her daughter June, and how it was most unattractive and of the worst yarn. I was so happy that she had become her usual self.

---

defeated   beaten

occasions   times, events

scalp   the skin on one's head

quivering   shaking, usually with strong emotion

stunned   shocked

scolding   criticizing, speaking angrily

porridge   hot cereal

But after I got well, I discovered that, really, my mother had changed. She no longer hovered over me as I practiced different chess games. She did not polish my trophies every day. She did not cut out the small newspaper item that mentioned my name. It was as if she had erected an invisible wall and I was secretly groping each day to see how high and how wide it was.

At my next tournament, while I had done well overall, in the end the points were not enough. I lost. And what was worse, my mother said nothing. She seemed to walk around with this satisfied look, as if it had happened because she had devised this strategy.

I was horrified. I spent many hours every day going over in my mind what I had lost. I knew it was not just the last tournament. I examined every move, every piece, every square. And I could no longer see the secret weapons of each piece, the magic within the intersection of each square. I could see only my mistakes, my weaknesses. It was as though I had lost my magic armor. And everybody could see this, where it was easy to attack me.

---

hovered   floated, hung
groping   feel about with the hands

horrified   very frightened or upset
intersection   place where two lines cross
armor   protective clothing for warfare

Over the next few weeks and later months and years, I continued to play, but never with that same feeling of supreme confidence. I fought hard, with fear and desperation. When I won, I was grateful, relieved. And when I lost, I was filled with growing dread, and then terror that I was no longer a prodigy, that I had lost the gift and had turned into someone quite ordinary.

When I lost twice to the boy whom I had defeated so easily a few years before, I stopped playing chess altogether. And nobody protested. I was fourteen.

---

desperation   hopelessness
dread   great fear
terror   total fear

protested   argued against, disagreed

ABOUT THE AUTHOR

Amy Tan was born in Oakland, California, two years after her parents immigrated to the U.S. from China. Following the deaths of her father and brother when she was 15, she left the U.S. and finished school in Montreux, Switzerland. She returned to the U. S., worked her way through college, and received her doctorate at the University of California at Berkeley. After her first visit to China in 1987, Tan said "It was just as my mother said: as soon as my feet touched China, I became Chinese."

➤ **Amy Tan (born 1952)** ◄

➤ *What Do You Think?*

Think about the story and discuss it with your classmates and your teacher. Below are some questions to get you started. In your discussion, try to use the text of the story to support your ideas.

1. What kind of chess player is the daughter at the beginning of the story? How do you know?
2. What kind of chess player is she at the end of the story? How do you know?
3. How does the mother feel about her daughter's chess playing at the beginning of the story? At the end?
4. How are the mother and the daughter in the story alike? How are they different?
5. In the game of chess, one player makes a move and then another player makes a move. How is this like the relationship between the daughter and the mother? What are the "moves" in their relationship that are described in the story? What are the "strategies," or game plans, of the mother and the daughter in the story?
6. How do the two characters change?
7. What lessons does the daughter learn?

➤ *Try This*

The Best Game Debate

1. Work in a group of four. Use an audio cassette recorder to tape your discussion.
2. Each person should tell the group about games he or she likes to play.
3. Discuss together which games you as a group think are the best. Each person should give reasons to defend his or her choices. Try to reach agreement on one game everyone likes to play.
4. Listen to the audiotape of your discussion.
5. From the tape recording, choose the most interesting minute of discussion. Try to choose a minute with many different speakers.
6. Transcribe, or write down, the one-minute discussion. Use the rules on the next page to write down speech.

➤ Learning About Literature

Dialogue

When an author transcribes the exact words of the characters' conversation, the author is using *dialogue*. Dialogue often adds to the interest of a selection because it can reveal the speech patterns and personality of a character, and it can show the events of a story from more than one point of view.

In strong writing, the author is able to "show" the reader the characters and the plot of the story rather than just "tell" about them. This makes the reader more interested, more imaginative, and more active in figuring out what is happening in the reading selection. Careful use of dialogue can help a writer make his or her writing come alive and draw the reader into the literature.

Choose a piece of dialogue from "Four Directions" that is especially interesting to you. Read it aloud to the class. Explain why you like the way the author has written that piece of dialogue.

➤ Writing

A Short Story with Dialogue AM

1. Write a short story about a topic you choose. Include some memorable characters.
2. Use a Story Map to outline your story's basic elements.
3. Use Character Maps to sketch out your characters.
4. Include dialogue to "show" what your characters are like rather than just "telling" your reader about the characters. Use the rules in the box titled *A Few Rules for Transcribing Speech* when you write dialogue.
5. Remember to use the steps of the writing process to share, edit, and revise your work.

A Few Rules for Transcribing Speech

1. Start a new paragraph each time a different person speaks.
2. Put quotation marks (" ") before and after the exact words a person uses.
3. If the person's words are in the middle of a sentence, put a comma before and after the quotation. The comma before the quote is outside the quotation marks (, "). The comma after the quote is inside the quotation marks (,").
4. If another punctuation mark is at the end of the quote, include it inside the quotation marks (!") (.").

   Look at examples in the story, "Four Directions."

➤ Exploring Your Own Experience

Tree of Hope

On a large piece of paper, one person should draw the outline of a tree with many branches. Cut out the tree and hang it up. Now, each student should write one hope he or she has for the future on a self-stick note. Share your hope with classmates. Place your hope note on the tree for a classroom display.

➤ Background

The following selection is taken from the poem that Maya Angelou read on January 20th, 1993, when William Jefferson Clinton became President of the United States.

On the Pulse of Morning

(excerpt) by
Maya Angelou

Lift up your eyes upon
This day breaking for you.
Give birth again
To the dream.

Women, children, men,
Take it into the palms of your hands,
Mold it into the shape of your most
Private need. Sculpt it into
The image of your most public self.
Lift up your hearts
Each new hour holds new chances
For new beginnings.
Do not be wedded forever
To fear, yoked eternally
To brutishness.

---

brutishness   animal-like roughness, rudeness, or violence

Men Exist for the Sake of One Another. Teach Them Then or Bear With Them by Jacob Lawrence, 1938

The horizon leans forward,
Offering you space
To place new steps of change.
Here, on the pulse of this fine day
You may have the courage
To look up and out and upon me,
The Rock, the River, the Tree, your country.
No less to Midas than the mendicant.

....

horizon   place where the sky meets the earth
pulse   heartbeat
no less   the same
Midas   legendary king whose touch turned things to gold
mendicant   beggar

No less to you now than the mastodon then.
Here on the pulse of this new day
You may have the grace to look up and out
And into your sister's eyes
And into your brother's face,
Your country,
And say simply
Very simply
With hope—
Good morning.

---

mastodon   prehistoric, elephant-like mammal
grace   goodwill, help of God

ABOUT THE AUTHOR

Maya Angelou, born Marguerite Johnson in St. Louis, Missouri, was raised with her grandparents in Arkansas. Her love for literature and language has led her to a varied career. She has published five volumes of her autobiography, five volumes of poetry, and several plays. Angelou has also toured Europe and Africa singing the lead role in the opera *Porgy and Bess,* and has written for newspapers in Ghana and Egypt.

➤ **Maya Angelou (born 1928)** ◄

➤ *What Do You Think?*

Think about the poem and discuss it with your classmates and your teacher. Below are some questions to get you started. In your discussion, try to use the text of the poem to support your ideas.

1. What time of day is it in the poem?
2. What does the poet ask the reader to do with "the dream?" What does she ask the reader not to do?
3. What do you think morning and the horizon *symbolize* in the poem? What do you think the rock, the river, and the tree symbolize?
4. Does the poet predict that building a hopeful future will be hard work? Why or why not? Find examples in the poem to support your ideas.
5. What is this poet's advice to the reader? Is it good advice? Why or why not?

➤ *Learning About Literature*

Powerful Verbs

Good writers choose powerful, interesting words to communicate their messages. They rarely use static or motionless verbs such as "is" or "was." When they can, they use stronger, more active verbs. Reread the stanzas from "On the Pulse of Morning" to look for the verbs Maya Angelou chooses. For example, in the first stanza, she uses three strong verbs: *"Lift* up your eyes upon / This day *breaking* for you. / *Give birth* again / to the dream." Make a list of powerful verbs you can find in the rest of the poem.

➤ Try This

Revising for Powerful Verbs

Choose a piece of your own writing that you like, but would like to make stronger. Look for forms of the verb *to be (am, is, are, was, were, have been, will be, would be,* and so on) and underline them. Replace them with stronger verbs. Use a dictionary, a thesaurus, and a translation dictionary whenever you need to. Read over your revision to see how much stronger and more interesting the writing is.

➤ Writing

Advice AM

1. Write about the hopes and dreams you have for yourself and the world.
2. Include advice on how to make those hopes and dreams come true.
3. Choose the form of writing you think best expresses your ideas—perhaps a poem, a story, or an essay.
4. Use the steps of the writing process to share, revise and polish your work.

Unit Follow–Up

➤ *Making Connections*

Unit Project Ideas **AM**

Here are some possible unit projects. You may choose to think up a project of your own and check it out with your teacher. Use some of the strategies and concepts you learned in the unit to help you plan and complete your project. These strategies and concepts include: ranking ladder, repetition, rhyme scheme, irony, scanning, humor, interviews, static and dynamic characterization, dialect, analogy, proverbs, idioms, round table, dialogue, writing process, and using powerful words.

1. **Character Comparisons.** Choose two characters in this unit to compare and contrast. You may choose to use a Venn diagram and/or a Character Web to help you get ready to write. You might like to include your own illustrations of what you think the characters look like.

2. **Rules for Interesting Writing.** Several ideas for making your writing more interesting have been included in this unit. Collect the ideas and summarize them in your own words. Publish a pamphlet of your own with a title like "Advice for Interesting Writing."

3. **Advice Chart.** In all of the selections in this unit, the author and/or characters offer some kind of advice. Make a display chart summarizing the advice and who offers it. Your chart might look something like the one below.

4. **Reviews.** Choose your favorite selection from this unit. Write a review in which you briefly tell what the selection is about. Try to discuss its strong and weak points, and then recommend it to others, telling why you think they might enjoy it. You also might consider comparing the selection with other works.

5. **Rhythm and Rhyme Schemes of Songs.** Write down the lyrics, or words, to two of your favorite songs. Scan, or mark, the lyrics to analyze their rhythm and their rhyme schemes. Remember to use accent marks to indicate accented and unaccented syllables. How do the rhythm and rhyme add to your enjoyment of these songs?

Advice in Unit 4		
Title	*Person Offering Advice*	*Advice*

6. Advice: A Play. Create a Reader's Theater play using one of the stories or poems in this unit, or, if you choose, write an original play in which a character offers advice to someone else. Perform the play for classmates. Videotape the production to show at parents' night or in other classes.

7. What Have I Learned? What Next? Review the table of contents in *Voices In Literature Gold*. Look for strategies, ideas, and terms you have learned from the book. Make a list of the things you have learned. Then make another list of what you want to learn next in your study of literature. Consult the "Further Reading" suggestions at the end of chapters and make a list of books you'd like to read soon. Then write a short paragraph about your goals for enjoying and learning more about literature.

Further Reading

Below are some books related to this unit that you might enjoy.

• *The Adventures of Connie and Diego / Las Aventuras de Connie y Diego,* by Maria Garcia. Children's Book Press, 1987. Short and brightly illustrated, this bilingual text offers, through a story, advice on how to live together in a multicultural world.

• *Black Boy,* by Richard Wright. Harper Perennial, 1945. This classic work depicts the struggles of growing up as an African- American in the first half of the nineteenth century.

• *The Joy Luck Club,* by Amy Tan. G. Putnam's Sons, 1989. The relationships between American-born daughters and their Chinese-born mothers are explored in this interesting novel.

• *On the Pulse of Morning,* by Maya Angelou. Random House, 1993. This book includes the complete text of the poem read by Angelou at President Clinton's inauguration in 1993.

• *Selected Poems of Langston Hughes,* by Langston Hughes. Random House, 1959. The poems in this collection, which were chosen by Hughes himself shortly before his death, span the poet's entire career.

• *Songs from This Earth on Turtle's Back,* edited by Joseph Bruchac. The Greenfield Review Press, 1983. Bruchac has assembled an outstanding collection of Native-American poems. Poets introduce their works with short autobiographical sketches.

• *The Spirit Walker,* by Nancy Wood. Doubleday, 1993. The wisdom of Native-Americans is celebrated and passed on in this collection of Wood's poems. Beautiful paintings of Native-Americans and their lands illustrate the poetry.

• *Stories from El Barrio,* by Piri Thomas. Alfred A. Knopf, 1978. Thomas' autobiographical stories tell of his youth with his Puerto Rican-American family in Spanish Harlem.

Remaining Text from *The Raven* and *Romeo and Juliet,* Act II, Scene 2

The Raven

by
Edgar Allan Poe

*Below are the stanzas from **"The Raven"** which do not appear in the excerpt on page 99.*

Much I marvelled this ungainly fowl to hear discourse so plainly,
Though its answer little meaning—little relevancy bore;
For we cannot help agreeing that no living human being
Ever yet was blessed with seeing bird above his chamber door,—
Bird or beast upon the sculptured bust above his chamber door—
    With such name as "Nevermore."

But the Raven, sitting lonely on the placid bust, spoke only
That one word, as if his soul in that one word he did outpour.
Nothing further then he uttered; not a feather then he fluttered,—
Till I scarcely more than muttered, "Other friends have flown before!
On the morrow *he* will leave me, as my hopes have flown before!"
    Then the bird said "Nevermore."

marvelled   was surprised at
discourse   talk
placid   calm
uttered   said

Startled at the stillness broken by reply so aptly spoken,
"Doubtless," said I, "what it utters is its only stock and store,
Caught from some unhappy master whom unmerciful Disaster
Followed fast and followed faster till his songs one burden bore,—
Till the dirges of his Hope that melancholy burden bore
　　Of 'Never,—nevermore.'"

But the Raven still beguiling all my sad soul into smiling,
Straight I wheeled a cushioned seat in front of bird, and bust and door;
Then, upon the velvet sinking, I betook myself to linking
Fancy unto fancy, thinking what this ominous bird of yore,—
What this grim, ungainly, ghastly, gaunt, and ominous bird of yore
　　Meant in croaking "Nevermore."

This I sat engaged in guessing, but no syllable expressing
To the fowl whose fiery eyes now burned into my bosom's core;
This and more I sat divining, with my head at ease reclining
On the cushion's velvet lining that the lamplight gloated o'er,
But whose velvet violet lining, with the lamplight gloating o'er,
She shall press, ah, nevermore!

---

unmerciful　without pity

dirges　funeral songs

melancholy　sad, gloomy

ominous　threatening, scary

yore　times past

ungainly　awkward, clumsy, unattractive

gaunt　very thin

divining　figuring out, anticipating

reclining　lying back

Then, methought, the air grew denser, perfumed from an unseen censer
Swung by Seraphim whose footfalls tinkled on the tufted floor.
"Wretch," I cried, "thy God hath lent thee—by these angels
he hath sent thee
Respite—respite and nepenthe from thy memories of Lenore!
Quaff, oh quaff this kind nepenthe and forget this lost Lenore!"
    Quoth the Raven, "Nevermore."

"Prophet!" said I, "thing of evil!—prophet still, if bird or devil!—
Whether Tempter sent, or whether tempest tossed thee here ashore,
Desolate yet all undaunted, on this desert land enchanted—
On this home by horror haunted—tell me truly, I implore—
Is there—*is* there balm in Gilead?—tell me!—tell me, I implore!"
    Quoth the Raven, "Nevermore."

"Prophet!" cried I, "thing of evil!—prophet still, if bird or devil!—
By that Heaven that bends above us—by that God we both adore!—

....

denser   thicker
censer   container for burning incense
Seraphim   angels of the highest order
tufted   carpeted
nepenthe   removing sorrow, also a drug said to cause forgetfulness of sorrow
quaff   drink
desolate   alone, barren
undaunted   fearless, confident
balm in Gilead   refers to a medicinal herb mentioned in the Bible

Tell this soul with sorrow laden if, within the distant Aidenn,
It shall clasp a sainted maiden whom the angels name Lenore—
Clasp a rare and radiant maiden whom the angels name Lenore."
    Quoth the Raven, "Nevermore."

"Be that word our sign of parting, bird or fiend!" I shrieked, upstarting.
"Get thee back into the tempest and the Night's Plutonian shore!
Leave no black plume as a token of that lie thy soul hath spoken
Leave my loneliness unbroken!—quit the bust above my door!
Take thy beak from out my heart, and take thy form from off my door!"
    Quoth the Raven, "Nevermore."

And the Raven, never flitting, still is sitting, still is sitting
On the pallid bust of Pallas just above my chamber door;
And his eyes have all the seeming of a demon's that is dreaming,
And the lamplight o'er him streaming throws his shadow on the floor;
And my soul from out that shadow that lies floating on the floor
    Shall be lifted—nevermore!

Aidenn   a Moslem paradise
radiant   shining, beautiful
fiend   devil
tempest   storm
plume   feather
flitting   flying lightly and quickly, like a butterfly
demon   devil

Balcony Scene from *Romeo and Juliet*

by
William Shakespeare

*Below are the stanzas from **"Romeo and Juliet, Act II, Scene 2"** which do not appear in the excerpt on page 157.*

Act II, Scene 2
ROMEO, JULIET

Juliet.

By whose direction found'st thou out this place?

Romeo.

By Love, that first did prompt me to inquire.
He lent me counsel, and I lent him eyes.
I am no pilot, yet, wert thou as far
As that vast shore washed with the farthest sea,
I would adventure for such merchandise.

Juliet.

Thou know'st the mask of night is on my face,
Else would a maiden blush bepaint my cheek,
For that which thou has heard me speak tonight.
Fain would I dwell on form, fain, fain deny
What I have spoke; but farewell compliment!

....

inquire   ask
fain   gladly, readily

Dost thou love me? I know thou wilt say "Ay,"
And I will take thy word. Yet if thou swear'st,
Thou may'st prove false. At lovers' perjuries,
They say, Jove laughs. O gentle Romeo,
If thou dost love, pronounce it faithfully,
Or if thou think'st I am too quickly won,
I'll frown and be perverse and say thee nay,—
So wilt thou woo: but else, not for the world.
In truth, fair Montague, I am too fond,
And therefore thou may'st think my 'havior light;
But trust me, gentleman, I'll prove more true
Than those that have more cunning to be strange.
I should have been more strange, I must confess,
But that thou overheard'st ere I was ware,
My true love's passion; therefore pardon me,
And not impute this yielding to light love,
Which the dark night hath so discovered.

Romeo.

Lady, by yonder blessed moon I vow,
That tips with silver all these fruit-tree tops—

---

ay   yes

perjuries   lies

Jove   the king of Roman gods, Jupiter

perverse   contrary, difficult

'havior   behavior, how one acts

cunning   wits, quickness of mind

ware   aware

impute   credit, assign

Juliet.

O, swear not by the moon, the inconstant moon,
That monthly changes in her circled orb,
Lest that thy love prove likewise variable.

Romeo.

What shall I swear by?

Juliet.

Do not swear at all.
Or, if thou wilt, swear by thy gracious self,
Which is the god of my idolatry,
And I'll believe thee.

Romeo.

                          If my heart' dear love—

Juliet.

Well, do not swear. Although I joy in thee,
I have no joy of this contract tonight;
It is too rash, too unadvis'd, too sudden,
Too like the lightning, which doth cease to be
Ere one can say "It lightens." Sweet, good night!
This bud of love, by summer's ripening breath,
May prove a beauteous flower when next we meet.
Good night, good night! As sweet repose and rest
Come to thy heart as that within my breast!

Romeo.

O, wilt thou leave me so unsatisfied?

....

contract   promise
rash   hurried
repose   sleep, peace

Juliet.

What satisfaction canst thou have tonight?

Romeo.

The exchange of thy love's faithful vow for mine.

Juliet.

I gave thee mine before thou didst request it;
And yet I would it were to give again.

Romeo.

Wouldst thou withdraw it? For what purpose, love?

Juliet.

But to be frank, and give it thee again.
And yet I wish but for the thing I have.
My bounty is as boundless as the sea,
My love as deep; the more I give to thee,
The more I have, for both are infinite.
(NURSE calls within.)
I hear some noise within; dear love, adieu!
Anon, good nurse! Sweet Montague, be true.
Stay but a little, I will come again. *(Exit.)*

Romeo.

O, blessed, blessed night! I am afeard,
Being in night, all this is but a dream,
Too flattering-sweet to be substantial.
(Re-enter JULIET, above.)

....

frank   honest, truthful
boundless   endless
substantial   actual, real

Juliet.

Three words, dear Romeo, and good night indeed.
If that thy bent of love be honorable,
Thy purpose marriage, send me word tomorrow,
By one that I'll procure to come to thee,
Where and what time thou wilt perform the rite;
And all my fortunes at thy foot I'll lay,
and follow thee my lord throughout the world.

Nurse.

(Within) Madam!

Juliet.

I come, anon. — But if thou meanst not well, I do beseech
thee —

Nurse.

(Within) Madam!

Juliet.

> By and by, I come: —

To cease thy suit, and leave me to my grief.
Tomorrow will I send.

Romeo.

> So thrive my soul —

....

rite   wedding
beseech   beg
cease thy suit   stop trying
thrive   grow, do very well

Juliet.

A thousand times good night! *(Exit)*

Romeo.

A thousand times the worse, to want thy light.
Love goes toward love, as schoolboys from their books,
But love from love, toward school with heavy looks.
(Retiring slowly.)
(Re-enter JULIET, above.)

Juliet.

Hist! Romeo, hist!—O, for a falconer's voice,
To lure this tassel-gentle back again!
Bondage is hoarse, and may not speak aloud;
Else would I tear the cave where Echo lies
And make her airy tongue more hoarse than mine
With repetition of my Romeo's name.

Romeo.

It is my soul that calls upon my name.
How silver-sweet sound lovers' tongues by night,
Like softest music to attending ears!

Juliet.

Romeo!

Romeo.

My dear?

Juliet.

      What o'clock tomorrow
Shall I send to thee?

---

bondage being tied up, restrained

Romeo.

By the hour of nine.

Juliet.

I will not fail; 'tis twenty years till then.
I have forgot why I did call thee back.

Romeo.

Let me stand here till thou remember it.

Juliet.

I shall forget, to have thee still stand there,
Remembering how I love thy company.

Romeo.

And I'll still stay, to have thee still forget,
Forgetting any other home but this.

Juliet.

'Tis almost morning. I would have thee gone; —
And yet no farther than a wanton's bird;
Who lets it hop a little from her hand,

....

wanton's   playful child's

Like a poor prisoner in his twisted gyves,
And with a silk thread plucks it back again,
So loving-jealous of his liberty.

Romeo.

I would, I were thy bird.

Juliet.

                Sweet, so would I;
Yet I should kill thee with much cherishing.
Good night, good night! Parting is such sweet sorrow
That I shall say good night till it be morrow. *(Exit.)*

Romeo.

Sleep dwell upon thine eyes, peace in thy breast!
Would I were sleep and peace, so sweet to rest!
Hence will I to my ghostly father's cell,
His help to crave and my dear hap to tell. *(Exit.)*

---

gyves   shackles, handcuffs attached to chains

APPENDIX B

GUIDE TO LITERARY TERMS AND TECHNIQUES

Alliteration   The repetition of beginning consonant sounds in a literary work (p. 165). See also **SOUND DEVICES**.

> EXAMPLE: "Shooting sparks into space."
> *(West Side Story,* pp. 147–155).

Analogy   An extended comparison showing how two things are alike (p. 194). In *Mother to Son,* Langston Hughes uses an analogy when he compares life to a stairway (pp. 191–193).

Anapestic foot   Two unstressed syllables followed by a stressed syllable. See also **FOOT** (p. 181).

> EXAMPLE: "Ĭf yŏu gŏ tŏ Dŭndée, ălwăys tăke lŏts ŏf téa."

Anecdote   A short account of an interesting event in someone's life. Anecdotes are often used to make a point, describe a person, or explain an idea. Anecdotes can be humorous or serious (p. 87).

Anonymous author   Unknown writer. The name of the author has been forgotten over time, or the author has chosen not to take credit for the work (p. 112).

Assonance   The repetition of vowel sounds in a literary work (p. 107). See also **SOUND DEVICES.**

> EXAMPLE: "A rare and radiant maiden whom the angels named Lenore," *(The Raven,* pp. 99–105).

Autobiography   A person's account of his or her own life (p. 209).

Biography   An account of a person's life written by another author. Most selections in *Voices in*

Literature Gold are followed by a short biography of the author (p. 133).

Blank verse   Poetry written with regular meter or rhythmic pattern, but unrhymed. Shakespeare used blank verse for many of his plays.

> EXAMPLE: "Bŭt sóft! Whăt líght thrŏugh yóndĕr wíndŏw breáks:
> Ĭt ís thĕ éast, ănd Júlĭĕt ís thĕ sún!"
> *(Romeo and Juliet,* pp. 157–163).

Cause and effect   Events in a narrative can be related by cause and effect. The cause is the event that happens first and is the reason something else happens. The change that takes place as a result is the effect. Sometimes an event that is an effect can then become the cause of another event (p. 44).

Character   The persons (or sometimes animals, things, or natural forces presented as persons) that appear in short stories, novels, plays, or narrative poems. See also **DYNAMIC CHARACTER** and **STATIC CHARACTER** (p. 187).

Character development   The way that a character changes, or develops, throughout a story. Authors can show character development by showing the character acting and speaking, by giving a physical description of the character, by telling the character's thoughts, by telling what other characters think about the character, and by directly describing the character (pp. 46, 165).

Cliché   Very common phrase (p. 199).

Climax   The moment of greatest tension or emotional intensity, interest, or suspense in a narrative or other literary work. It is sometimes called the *crisis* or *turning point* (p. 44). See also **PLOT** (p. 46).

Compare and contrast   An effective way to study literature is to compare, or find things that are the same, and to contrast, or find things that are different in various elements of literary works (pp. 86, 165).

Conclusion   The ending of a piece of writing. Since the conclusion leaves the last impression on a reader, good writers take care to make the conclusion strong and memorable (p. 123).

Conflict   A struggle between characters, things, or ideas that oppose, or seem to fight against one another, in a work of literature. Conflict can take place between persons, between a person and society, between a person and nature, or between two ideas within a person (p. 143). In *The Sullivan Ballou Love Letter,* the writer reveals the strong conflict Ballou feels between love for his wife and love for his country (pp. 137–141).

Contrast   To find differences in elements of literary works (p. 144). See also **COMPARE AND CONTRAST** (pp. 86–165).

Dactylic foot   A stressed syllable followed by two unstressed syllables. See also **FOOT** (p. 181).

EXAMPLE: "Raíndrŏps ŏn rósĕs ănd whiskĕrs ŏn kittĕns".

Description   Details of a person, place, thing, or event used both in prose and poetry to re-create sensory impressions—sights, sounds, smells, textures, tastes. Descriptions can be factual or can be used to set a mood or evoke an emotion (p. 129).

Dialect   Forms of speech used in a region of a country, or by a particular group of people, which use sentence patterns, vocabulary, and pronunciation that differ from standard speech (pp. 190, 195). Langston Hughes uses an African-American dialect in *Mother to Son* (pp. 191–193).

Dialogue   The exact words used in characters' conversations. Dialogue is an effective way for writers to "show, not tell" characterizations or plot events in the story, and thus engage the reader. In prose or poetry, dialogue is usually marked with quotation marks. In drama, dialogue is indicated by the speaking character's name before his or her "lines" (p. 221).

Drama   A story acted out, usually on a stage, by people playing the parts of the characters. Two types of drama are comedies and tragedies. *Comedies* are plays that end happily and often use humor. *Tragedies* are dramas in which the main characters meet with an unhappy ending, as happened in *Romeo and Juliet* (pp. 157–163, pp. 234–241).

Dramatic irony   When the reader or the audience knows something that a character does not know (p. 17). An example of dramatic irony in the play *Romeo and Juliet* is the moment when Romeo thinks Juliet is dead and kills himself. However, the audience knows that Juliet is still alive (pp. 157–163, pp. 234–241).

Dynamic character   A character that experiences some change in personality or attitude in a narrative (p. 187). For example, in *The Raiders Jacket,* Lorena's ideas about what is important change as a result of her experiences throughout the story (pp. 33–43). See also **CHARACTER**.

Essay   A form of writing in which the writer takes a clear stand on an issue. A *formal essay* is an attempt to inform, teach, or convince the reader. It has a serious tone, presents its arguments logically using persuasive writing. An *informal essay* is a lighter piece that usually attempts to entertain the reader and often has a looser structure (p. 53).

Event   Something that happens in a story. A series of events make up the plot, or story line, of a narrative (p. 44).

Fiction   Any writing that is invented, imagined, or untrue. Fiction is usually prose or a narrative (p. 65).

APPENDIX B

Figurative Language Language that is not meant to be understood in a literal sense, but rather makes use of comparisons between different things (p. 196). See also METAPHOR, SIMILE.

Flashback A scene in narrative fiction, narrative poetry, or drama in which the time order of a story is interrupted by the telling of an event that happened in the past (p. 44). In *The Raiders Jacket,* the story begins on Saturday, and then there is a flashback to events that occurred on Wednesday that led up to Saturday's problems (pp. 33–43).

Folktale A special kind of short story which originated from people who could neither read nor write, and which was passed from person to person by the spoken word. Folktales often contain heroes or heroines, adventure, magic, or romance. Because folktales were passed on through the oral tradition, there are often many versions of the same story (p. 81). *A Mother's Advice* (pp. 183–185) and *The Wise Woman of Córdoba* (pp. 75–79) are examples of folktales.

Foot A basic unit of meter that gives a poem, or part of a poem, a particular beat. See also IAMBIC FOOT, TROCHAIC FOOT, DACTYLIC FOOT, AND ANAPESTIC FOOT (p. 181).

Foreshadowing The use of clues in narrative to suggest events that have not yet happened. Foreshadowing helps to build suspense in a story and helps the reader focus on important details as suspense builds (p. 81). In the first paragraph of *The Wife's Story* (pp. 89–95), Ursula Le Guin foreshadows a tragic ending.

Free verse Verse without a set rhythmic pattern, but rather the natural rhythms of speech. Free verse can be rhymed or unrhymed. Like the rhythms in natural speech, rhythms in free verse can change at any time, and lines can be of different lengths (pp. 73, 130). Carl Sandburg, (pp. 131–133) Maya Angelou, (pp. 223–225) Langston Hughes, (pp.

191–193) Piri Thomas, (pp. 201–209), and Joy Harjo (pp. 171–173) all use free verse.

Iambic foot An unstressed syllable followed by a stressed syllable. See also FOOT (p. 181).

EXAMPLE: "Tŏníght, tŏníght, Ĭ'll śee m̆y lóve tŏníght." *(West Side Story,* pp. 147–155).

Idiom An interesting phrase or expression whose meaning can not be understood by literally interpreting the words in it (p. 210).

EXAMPLES: "It's raining cats and dogs." (It's raining very hard.) *(The Raiders Jacket,* pp. 33–43). "He stopped on a dime." (He stopped quickly.) *(La Peseta,* pp. 201–209).

Imagery Language that appeals to any of the five senses—sight, sound, touch, smell, taste—or to a combination of these senses. Poets and other writers use imagery to create vivid, or clear images (p. 114).

Inference When a reader has ideas about a story that use information from the story but are not directly stated, the reader is making inferences (p. 66).

Irony A contrast or a lack of "fit" between what is stated in a literary work and what is meant, or between what is expected to happen and what really happens. See also VERBAL IRONY, DRAMATIC IRONY, and SITUATIONAL IRONY (p. 17).

Lead The opening or beginning of a selection. A strong lead sets the tone and catches the interest of the reader (p. 123). For example, Huynh Quang Nhyong, in the lead of *Karate,* introduces a possible conflict: "My grandmother had married a man whom she loved with all her heart, but who was totally different from her" (pp. 117–121).

Literal language   Non-figurative language which directly states facts or ideas (p. 196).

Lyric poetry   Poetry that expresses the poet's personal emotions or sentiments rather than telling of events. Love poems, patriotic songs and odes are all examples of lyric poetry (p. 211).

Memoir   A writer's recollection of an earlier life experience (p. 10).

Metaphor   A figure of speech in which a writer describes something by calling it something else (p. 134).

> EXAMPLE: "Love is a sea where phantom ships cross always." (*Solo for Saturday Night Guitar*, pp. 131–133).

Meter   A rhythmic pattern that repeats itself over and over in a line of writing. The number and kind of feet in a line determine the meter. See also **FOOT** (p. 181).

Narration   Writing that tells a story. This writing moves from event to event, usually in chronological, or time, order. Short stories, novels, poems, and plays can all use narration (p. 211).

Narrative   Writing that is in story form (p. 67).

Narrative poetry   Poetry that tells a story (p. 211). *La Peseta,* by Piri Thomas, is an example of a narrative poem (pp. 201–209).

Narrator   One who tells, or narrates, a story. A story can be narrated in the first person or the third person. *La Peseta,* (pp. 201–209) and *Eleven,* (pp. 11–15) are stories told by a first-person narrator; *The Raiders Jacket* (pp. 33–43), is told by a third-person narrator. The author can also serve as narrator as in, *A Mother's Advice.* (pp. 183–185). See also **POINT OF VIEW** (p. 97).

News article   A selection that presents the facts of a situation, usually without taking sides. News articles answer basic factual questions about an event, such as "Who?", "What?", "When?", "Where?", "How?", and "Why?" (p. 53).

Nonfiction   Prose narrative that tells about actual events or presents factual information. *The Dress Mess* (pp. 49–51) is an example of nonfiction writing.

Ode   A special form of poetry that praises someone or something enthusiastically. Poets throughout history have written odes in praise of heroes, famous people, works of art, and nature's power and beauty (p. 24).

Parallelism   Repetition of phrases, clauses, or sentences that are similar in structure or meaning (p. 114). In *Remember,* Joy Harjo begins most lines with the command "Remember..." (pp. 171–173).

Paraphrase   A summary of a literary work that tells in the simplest form what happened (p.106).

Playwright   The author of a drama or play (p. 163). See also **DRAMA.**

Plot   The main events or story line of a narrative. Plot usually includes these parts: *Exposition*, *rising action*, *climax* (crisis, or turning point), *falling action,* and *resolution* (or dénouement) (p. 46). See also **CLIMAX, RESOLUTION.**

Poetic license   A poet's right to break rules of form, grammar, punctuation, usage, and logic and to deviate from facts for artistic effect (pp. 68).

Poetry   Traditional poetry is language arranged in lines with regular rhythm and often rhyme. Non-traditional poetry is also usually set up in lines, but does not have regular rhythm or rhyme. Poetry is recognized by rich, dense language, powerful sounds, and evoking strong feelings in the reader (p. 9).

Point of view   The relationship of the storyteller to the story. The three basic points of view are the *first person point of view, the limited third person point of view,* and *the omniscient point of view.*

In the *first person point of view*, the narrative is told by one of the characters from the "I" point of view. This point of view is limited because the reader knows only what the character narrating knows. In the *third person point of view*, the narrator tells the story using "he" and "she." This point of view can be *limited*, with the narrator knowing only the thoughts and feelings of one character, or *omniscient*, with the narrator knowing the thoughts and feelings of all the characters (p. 97).

Prose   Written or spoken language that is not poetry. In *Eleven*, Sandra Cisneros uses very effective prose (pp. 11–15).

Proverb   A short popular saying that expresses some useful thought, popular belief, or truth (p. 196).

Repetition   A device used to emphasize the importance of words and phrases, often used in persuasive writing and poetry. Words, sounds, phrases, and patterns can be repeated (p. 9). See also PARALLELISM, ALLITERATION, ASSONANCE, AND RHYME.

Resolution   The outcome of the conflict of a play or story. Also called the dénoument. See also PLOT (p. 46).

Rhyme   The use of similar sounds in words or phrases that appear close to one another in a poem. Most rhymes are on the final syllable of the last word on a line.

> EXAMPLE: "Tonight, tonight
> The world is full of light,"
> (*West Side Story*, pp. 147–155).

Rhyming couplet   Two lines of a poem that appear together and that rhyme at the end (p. 22).

> EXAMPLE: "We sing, but oh the clay is vile
> Beneath our feet, and long the mile;" (*We Wear the Mask*, pp. 19–21).

Rhythm   The arrangement of *stressed* and *unstressed syllables* into a pattern. In English, stressed syllables are usually pronounced louder and clearer. Unstressed syllables are usually pronounced softer, and the vowel sound often changes to the unaccented vowel sound ("uh" or schwa.) In good writing, the stress or accent is on the important words. Poets, and sometimes prose writers as well, use words with similarly accented syllables to create rhythm. When the rhythm of a poem has a regular pattern, the pattern is called *meter*. In *The Raven* (pp. 99–105), Poe uses a very strong and consistent meter. See also METER, FOOT, FREE VERSE.

Setting   The time and place of the action of a narrative or story. In short stories, poetry, novels and nonfiction, the author usually creates the setting by description. In drama, the setting is usually created through stage directions and dialogue (p. 96).

Short story   A short prose narrative that can usually be read in one sitting. Short stories usually have the following elements: *plot, characterization, setting, point of view, theme,* and *style* (pp. 43, 221).

Simile   A figure of speech in which a writer compares two things, connecting them by "like" or "as" (p. 16).

> EXAMPLE: "...the way you grow old is kind of like an onion..."
> (*Eleven*, pp. 11–15).

Situational irony   An event that happens contrasts with what the characters, the readers, or the audience expect. For example, it would be situational irony if a firehouse burned down, or if a police station were robbed (p. 17).

Soliloquy   A literary discourse where a character speaks to himself/herself out loud (p. 164).

Sound devices   Ways of combining similar sounds for a poetic effect. See also ALLITERATION, ASSONANCE, METER, PARALLELISM, and REPETITION.

Speaker   The voice of a piece of literature. The speaker can be the author or a character created by the author. Identifying the speaker in a poem is a key to understanding the poem's meaning (p. 114).

Stanza   A group of lines forming a unit in a poem. Many poems have about 2–8 stanzas with a fixed pattern and rhyme. In other poems, stanzas vary in length and pattern and may or may not include rhyme (p. 73).

Static character   A character that remains the same throughout a narrative (p. 187). Often characters in folktales such as *A Mother's Advice* are static (pp. 183–185). See also **CHARACTER.**

Style   A writer's characteristic way of writing. Images, tone, and choice of literary devices all contribute to style. e. e. cummings' style, for example, is known for its lack of conventional form, punctuation, and its imaginative use of space on the page (pp. 69–71).

Suspense   The quality of a story that gives the reader a state of uncertainty that may make the reader feel anxious or eager to find out what will happen (p. 67).

Symbol   A person, place, thing, or action that has meaning in itself but also stands for something larger. The symbol may stand for a quality, a belief, or a value. A flag, for example, could be a symbol for love of one's country; a rose could be a symbol for love; a stairway could be a symbol for a climb through life (p. 226).

Synopsis   A brief summary of a piece of writing (p. 98).

Theme   The main idea or meaning of a literary work (p. 16). The theme is not the same as the subject. For example, the subject of Elizabeth Ruiz's poem, *Conceit,* is conceit, but the theme might be, "How we act determines how beautiful we are" (p. 197).

Theme statement   Sentence or sentences that express the main idea of a piece of writing (p. 52).

Thesis statement   Opening sentence of an essay that clearly explains what idea the writer will support in the essay (p. 189).

Tone   The attitude the author takes toward the subject, characters, and readers in a literary work. Writers can use tone to amuse, frighten, shock, or arouse compassion in readers. In *On the Pulse of Morning,* Maya Angelou conveys a very dignified, yet challenging tone (pp. 223–225). In *La Peseta,* Piri Thomas is sometimes playful, yet sometimes very serious in tone (pp. 201–209).

Trochaic foot   A stressed syllable followed by an unstressed syllable. See also **FOOT.**

EXAMPLES: "Dó nǒt sít ǒn áncǐent úncǐes..." (*Rules,* pp. 177–179). "Ońce ǔpón ǎ mídnǐght dřeařy, ás Ǐ pónderěd wéak and wéařy..." (*The Raven,* pp. 99–105).

Voice   Whoever is speaking in a poem (p. 143). See also **SPEAKER.**

Verbal irony   A writer or speaker says one thing and means another. For example, when something bad happens, people use irony when they say, "Oh, that's great" (p. 17).

APPENDIX C

Glossary

Many of the words in this Glossary have several meanings. The definitions we have used are the ones in the context in which the word appears in the book.

a

accelerating   speeding up
adorned   decorated, made pretty
Aidenn   a Moslem paradise
ancient   very old
anxious   worried
armor   protective clothing for warfare
arouse   awaken
arrested   taken to jail
assumed   something that is believed but not proven
astonishing   surprising
Athabaskan   a group of North-American Indians
authorities   persons in charge
ay   yes

b

bacalaito   *(Spanish)* salt cod fish
balm in Gilead   refers to a medicinal herb mentioned in the Bible
barrels   large, cylinder-shaped containers
barriers   blocks, walls
basin   wash bowl
beguiling   tricking
benefits   good results
benevolent associations   organizations that try to create good will toward a group of people
bescreen'd   hidden
beseech   beg
bestrides   sits upon, as on a horse
bewildered   lost, confused
blissful   very happy
bondage   being tied up, restrained

bound   held back, restrained
boundless   endless
braille   method of writing for the blind that uses raised dots
brandished   waved in a threatening manner
breeze   gentle wind
brutishness   animal-like roughness, rudeness, or violence
buenas noches   *(Spanish)* good night
bundles   bunches, groups of something tied together
bust   sculpture of head and shoulders

c

cabeza   *(Spanish)* head
cables   strong wires
cállate   *(Spanish)* be quiet
cannons   very large guns that shoot iron balls
caresses   touches lovingly
cash-strapped   with little money
cast down   feeling bad
cease thy suit   stop trying
censer   container for burning incense
centavos   *(Spanish)* cents
chamber   room
cherish   care for tenderly, treat carefully
chores   tasks, jobs around the house
chump   foolish person
clad   dressed
cleaver   large kitchen knife
clumsy   without grace, awkward
clutching   holding tightly
collapsed   fell down
como gatos y perros   *(Spanish)* like cats and dogs, very hard
competition   one trying to be better than another
compliance   cooperation, obedience

conceit pride, vanity, thinking highly of oneself

confide tell secretly

confidence faith in oneself

conjugate to list the forms of a verb

contract promise

corazón (Spanish) heart

counsel words, speech

countenance the way one holds oneself, the look on one's face

cowering hiding or hanging back in fear

craven coward

crematory place where the bodies of the dead are burned

crest feathers on a bird's head

cringed hung back, hid

crystal very clear, bright glass

cunning wits, quickness of mind

currently at present, now

curse evil spell or charm

cut turned a sharp corner

cynicism hopelessness, pessimism

d

dabbed patted

debris trash

decorum manner

decrepit old, falling apart

defeated beaten

demon devil

denser thicker

descendant child, grandchild, great-grandchild, etc.

desolate alone, barren

desperation hopelessness

destiny fate, future

determined resolved, set

devastating crushing, very harmful

devised created, made up

dinero (Spanish) money

dirges funeral songs

discourses speaks, converses

dissecting cutting apart to study

distinctly clearly

Divine Providence gifts or goodness of God

divining figuring out

doff take off, as a hat

doth does

dove jumped head-first into something

dread great fear

dreary dark and dull

drowsy sleepy

dying ember coal about to burn out

e

ebony black

echoed repeated back a sound

economic financial, money-related

economical money-saving

emblazoned decorated, displayed very brightly

enamored of being very fond of, liking very much

enmity hatred

entreat beg

envious jealous

errand short trip for a specific purpose

esa (Spanish) pal

evidence proof

f

fain gladly, readily

faltered hesitated, stopped for a minute

fantastically amazingly, unbelievably

fatally deadly

feel impelled feel the need

fern a non-flowering plant with feather-shaped leaves

fiend devil

flaca (Spanish) thin girl

flit fly lightly and quickly, like a butterfly

fondled stroked, petted

forelegs front legs of an animal

frank honest, truthful

frantic very upset, excited

frisk search a person by feeling his or her clothing

fulfilled granted, made happen

APPENDIX C

g

game   animals killed by hunters
gaunt   very thin
generosity   kindness, giving nature
gestures   points
ghastly   ghostlike
glaring   brightly shining, so much as to hurt one's eyes
goblins   evil or mischievous spirits, usually small and ugly
gordita   *(Spanish)* little, chubby girl. In Spanish, this is a complementary and affectionate term
got to bust out   *(slang)* has to break loose or get away
grace   goodwill, help of God
gradually   bit by bit, slowly
grave   solemn, serious, not funny
grief   deep sadness
grins   smiles widely
groping   feel about with the hands
grouch   complain in an unpleasant manner
guile   trickery
gyves   shackles, handcuffs attached to chains

h

hastening   hurrying, coming quickly
haven   safe place
'havior   behavior, how one acts
herbs   plants from which leaves and stems are used as medicines or seasonings
hesitation   pausing, waiting
horizon   place where the sky meets the earth
horrified   very frightened or upset
hosts   homes
hovered   floated, hung
how cam'st thou hither?   how did you come here?

i

I'se   I'm
I'se been a-climbin'   I've been climbing

ignorance   not knowing
immense   very big
impulse   sudden urge to do something
impute   credit, assign
incident   happening, event
indications   signs, clues
inhaling   breathing in
inheritance   money passed down by family
initially   at first
innocence   state of being not guilty or free from wrongdoing
inquire   ask
inteligente   *(Spanish)* smart, intelligent
intent   serious about something
intersection   place where two lines cross
intruder   unwanted person, meddler
irrevocable   final, irreversible

j

jests   makes jokes
Jove   the king of Roman gods, Jupiter
justifying   defending, making it sound right

k

kinder   kind of
kinsmen   relatives
Kiowa   Native-American tribe from the southwestern U.S. They once hunted buffalo and were fierce warriors.

l

larking   walking light-heartedly or playfully
lattice   crossed strips of metal or wood over an opening
leaping   jumping
lest   in case, should
loco   *(Spanish)* crazy
lore   learning

m

magnificent   very grand, impressive
majority   more than half

maldita *(Spanish)* cursed, evil

mane neck hair of an animal

marvelled was surprised at

mastodon prehistoric, elephant-like mammal

meager small, scant

melancholy sad, gloomy

mendicant beggar

mensa *(Spanish)* fool

mi carnal *(Spanish)* my brother

Midas legendary king whose touch turned things to gold

miners workers who dig up minerals such as coal, iron, gold, or silver from underground

mien manner

misgivings doubts, second thoughts

momentito *(Spanish)* just a minute

moped a bicycle with a motor

moral message, meaning

morrow next day, tomorrow

mortal fear fear for one's life

mortals human beings

motives reasons for doing things

mourn feel sorrow or sadness for someone who has died

murmured spoke in soft, rhythmic tone

myriad countless, many

n

nado, nadas, nada, nadamos, nadan *(Spanish)* I swim, you swim *(familiar)*, you swim *(formal)*, or he/she swims, we swim, they swim or you *(all)* swim

nagging complaining about the same thing over and over again

nepenthe removing sorrow, also a drug said to cause forgetfulness of sorrow

no less the same

nonetheless anyway

norm usual way of doing something

nostril nose hole

numb without feeling

o

o'er over

o'erperch climb over

obeisance bow

occasions times, events

Olé, olé *(Spanish)* "hurray!", a Spanish cheer

ominous threatening, scary

Omnipotence the all-powerful God

p

Pallas Pallas Athene, Greek goddess of wisdom

peered looked

peril danger

perjuries lies

perpetually without end, forever

perverse contrary, difficult

petal part of a flower blossom

phantom ghost

piercing deeply felt

placid calm

pleading begging

plume feather

Plutonian of the underworld, ruled by Pluto, or Hades, the god of the lower regions

pondered thought about

porridge hot cereal

pouch small bag for carrying things

pounce jump on something quickly

prisms pieces of glass shaped to turn light into rainbows

privileged people having money and advantages

proceeded went forward, continued

proclaiming announcing, stating loudly

profit a gaining of money

prorogued ended

protested argued against, disagreed

PTO Parent-Teacher Organization

pulse heartbeat

q

quaff   drink
quaint   strange, pleasantly different, unusual
qué guapo   *(Spanish)* how handsome
quivering   shaking, usually with strong emotion
quoth   said, quoted

r

radiant   shining, beautiful
rascal   scoundral, troublemaker
rash   hurried
reclining   lying back
relentlessly   without stopping
remorse   sorrow, regret
repose   sleep, peace
respond   answer
retraced   went back over
revive   wake up, bring back to consciousness
rifled   dug, searched
rite   wedding
rotten   old and spoiled, bad smelling
rouse   start to wake up or get up
rustling   sound of fabric rubbing together

s

sacrifice   give up
scalp   the skin on one's head
scarce   hardly
scolding   criticizing, speaking angrily
scuttling   moving quickly, as away from danger
sear   burn mark
sedan chair   enclosed chair supported on two poles used to carry a person
seraphim   angels of the highest order
shimmering   shining, sparkling like water at night
shivers   involuntary shaking caused by cold or fear
shorn   cut off
Sí, ya vengo   *(Spanish)* Yes, I'm coming now
siege   a persistent attack

sincere   true, honest
slaughter   killing, as in animals for food
snarled   made an angry, growling sound bearing teeth
sojourn   trip, journey
Sokoya   aunt, mother's sister
sparks   glowing pieces thrown off from a fire
species   types of animals or plants
sphere   shaped like a globe
spit   stick used for cooking meat over an open fire
splinters   small, thin, sharp pieces of wood
steered   guided in a certain direction
stiff   rigid, formal
stir   movement
stopped on a dime   *(idiom)* stopped very quickly
strategy   plan of attack
struggled   fought, worked hard for
stubble   short growth of beard
stunned   shocked
substantial   actual, real
subtleties   ways that are indirect, not open or easily detected
sultan   an Islamic ruler or prince
supreme   total, maximum, complete
surcease   end

t

te adoro   *(Spanish)* I love you
tempest   storm
temple   the side of the face next to the eye
temptation   desire to do something one shouldn't do
terror   terrible fear
thrive   grow, do very well
throbbing   pulsating, like a heartbeat
thrusting   shoving, sticking out
tiller   device used to steer a ship
toad   small, frog-like amphibian that lives on land
tokens   souvenirs, signs
tortured   hurt, tormented
trabajo   *(Spanish)* work

triumph success, victory
tufted carpeted
tweeds clothing of rough wool fabric
twitchy with quick, uncontrollable movements

u

ulterior hidden
undaunted fearless, confident
undetected not found out, undiscovered
ungainly awkward, clumsy, unattractive
unmerciful without pity
uttered said

v

vainly unsuccessfully
vestal pure, virgin
vigorous strong
vile hateful
volume book
voluntary personal choice
volunteer offer to do something

w

wafted floating on air
wag wave
waned faded, gotten smaller
wanton's playful child's
ware aware
wart small hard growth on the skin
wavering moving back and forth
weary tired
weaving moving back and forth
wherefore art thou where are you
whimpered cried softly
whine complain in a high nasal tone
wisp a small piece or strand
wond'ring wondering, questioning
wormed crawled or crept, wiggled
wrested pulled away, usually after a struggle
wretched pitiful, miserable, mean
wriggle move back and forth quickly
wrought shaped, made

y

yacht large, fancy sailing boat
yearning wanting, longing
yer your
yonder distant
yore times past

z

Zorro Mexican T.V. and film character

ACKNOWLEDGMENTS

Text

Unit 1

5 "My moccasins have not walked" by Duke Redbird from *Red on White: The Biography of Duke Redbird* by Marty Dunn. Copyright © 1971. Reprinted by permission of Stoddart Publishing, Don Mills, Ontario.

11 "Eleven" by Sandra Cisneros from *Woman Hollering Creek* by Sandra Cisneros. Reprinted by permission of The Bergholz Agency.

25 "Ode to My Socks" by Pablo Neruda. Reprinted from *Neruda and Vallejo: Selected Poems*, Beacon Press, Boston, 1971. Copyright © 1971 by Robert Bly. Reprinted with his permission.

33 "The Raiders Jacket" from *Local News*, Copyright © 1993 by Gary Soto. Reprinted by permission of Harcourt Brace & Company.

49 "The Dress Mess" by Del Stover. Reprinted with permission, from The American Board Journal, June. Copyright © 1990, the National School Boards Association. All rights reserved.

Unit 2

59 "The Ghost's Bride" by Laurence Yep from *The Rainbow People* by Laurence Yep. Copyright © 1989 by Laurence Yep. Reprinted by permission of HarperCollins Publishers.

69 "hist whist" by e.e. cummings. Reprinted by permission of Liveright Publishing Corporation, New York, New York.

75 "The Wise Woman of Córdoba" from *The Old Lady Who Ate People* by Francisco Hinojosa; illustrated by Leonel Maciel. Copyright © 1981 by Organización Editorial Novaro, S.A.; English Translation Copyright © 1984 by Organizatión Editorial Novaro, S.A. Reprinted by permission of Little, Brown and Company.

83 "The Hitchhiker" story, Korean Version by Haruo Aoki. Originally published in *The Vanishing Hitchhiker* by Jan Harold Brunvand.

85 "The Vanishing Hitchhiker" story, North Carolina Version by Douglas J. McMillan. Originally published in *The Vanishing Hitchhiker* by Jan Harold Brunvand. Reprinted by permission of the author, Douglas J. McMillan.

89 "The Wife's Story," copyright © 1982 by Ursula K. Le Guin; first appeared in *Changes*, ed. by Michael Bishop. Reprinted by permission of the author and the author's agent, Virginia Kidd.

Unit 3

117 "Karate" by Huynh Quang Nhuong from *The Land I Lost* by Huynh Quang Nhuong. Copyright © 1982 by Huynh Quang Nhuong. Reprinted by permission of HarperCollins Publishers.

125 "There Is No Word For Goodbye" by Mary TallMountain. Reprinted by permission of the author, Mary TallMountain.

131 "Solo for Saturday Night Guitar" from *Honey and Salt*, copyright © 1958 by Carl Sandburg and renewed 1986 by Margaret Sandburg, Helga Sandburg Crile and Janet Sandburg. Reprinted by permission of Harcourt Brace & Company.

147 Balcony Scene from *West Side Story* by Arthur Laurents and Stephen Sondheim. Copyright © 1957 by Leonard Bernstein and Stephen Sondheim. Copyright © 1956, 1958 by Arthur Laurents, Leonard Bernstein, Stephen Sondheim, and Jerome Robbins. Reprinted by permission of Random House, Inc.

Unit 4

171 "Remember" by Joy Harjo from the book *She Had Some Horses* by Joy Harjo. Copyright © 1983 by Joy Harjo. Used by permission of the publisher, Thunder's Mouth Press.

177 "Rules" by Karla Kuskin from the book *Dogs and Dragons, Trees and Dreams* by Karla Kuskin. Copyright ©1980 by Karla Kuskin. Reprinted by permission of HarperCollins Publishers.

ACKNOWLEDGMENTS

Nihonbashi Tori I-chome by Utwagawa Hiroshige (1797-1858), Edo period, Ansei era, 8/1858, Woodblock print, H13" W: 8 3/4", The Brooklyn Museum X896.44, Source unknown; **121** Courtesy HarperCollins Publishers; **126** Superstock; **127** Photo courtesy Kitty Costello; **132** The Granger Collection, 381 Park Ave. South, NYC 10016; **133** Photofest; **138** *Trooper Meditating Beside a Grave* by Winslow Homer, Joslyn Art Museum, Omaha, NE, JAM.1960.298, oil on canvas, ca. 1865; Gift of Dr. Harold Gifford and Ann Gifford Forbes; **140** Photo courtesy of the Atlanta History Center; **148** Comstock, Inc.; **152** Photofest; **155** Leonard Bernstein, courtesy of The Image Works; Steven Sondheim, courtesy of Wide World Photos; **158** Wide World Photos; **163** *The Flower Portrait of Shakespeare*, The Shakespeare Memorial Gallery at Stratford/Photofest; **168-169** Lithograph, edition of 175, Courtesy Estate of Romare Bearden; **172** Courtesy The Minnesota Historical Society; **173** Photo by Paul Abdoo; **178** The Granger Collection, 381 Park Ave. South, NYC 10016; **179** Photo by Nick Kuskin, courtesy HarperCollins Publishers; **184** Hermitage, St. Petersburg, Russia. Scala/Art Resources, NY; **192** Courtesy of The National Museum of American Art, Washington, D.C./Art Resources, NY; **193** Archive Photos; **197** Superstock; **202** Courtesy of The National Museum of American Art, Washington, D.C./Art Resources, NY, 1965.18.12, partial image of original; **206** Reproduction authorized by the Olga and Rufino Tamayo Foundation, A.C., Mexico City, Mexico; **209** Courtesy of The Shomburg Center for Research in Black Culture, The New York Public Library, NY; **214** Photo by Phil Bray, Courtesy Motion Picture & T.V. Archives; **216** Partial image of *Ladies Playing Double Sixes*. Courtesy of the Freer Gallery of Art, Smithsonian Institution, Washington, D.C.; 39.37/60.4: style of Chou Fang. China, Song Dynasty, 10th /11th Century. Ink and colors on silk, 30.7 x 69.4; **219** Wide World Photos; **224** Courtesy of The National Museum of American Art, Washington, D.C./Art Resources, NY; **225** Wide World Photos.